# A GLANCE
# OF
# HEAVEN

Richard Sibbes

*Vintage Puritan Series*
GLH Publishing
LOUISVILLE, KY

Sourced from *The Complete Works of Richard Sibbes.* Vol. IV.
Edited by Alexander Grosart. James Nichol, Edinburgh: 1863.

ISBN:
  Paperback 978-1-941129-83-8

# CONTENTS

To The Christian Reader ................................................ 1

The First Sermon............................................................ 3

The Second Sermon ..................................................... 17

The Third Sermon ........................................................ 37

The Fourth Sermon ...................................................... 57

# TO THE CHRISTIAN READER

Beloved! it is grown a custom that every book whosever, or of whatsoever subject, must be presented to you in state; with some prescript purposely. Were it not that custom is a tyrant, this labour might now be spared. Such matter from such an elder as here follows, needs no 'epistle of recommendation.' The reverend author is well approved to be 'a man of God,' a 'seer in Israel,' by those things which, without control, have already passed the press. Might I have my wish, it should be no more but a 'double portion' of that Spirit of God which was in him. The divine light, which radiated into his breast, displays itself in many other of his labours, but yet it is nowhere more condensed than in this following. It is truly said of Moses, by faith 'he saw him that was invisible,' Heb. xi. 27.

And St Paul prays for the Ephesians, 'that they might know the love of that which passeth knowledge,' Eph. iii. 19. These things imply a contradiction. Yet in like phrase I fear not to say of this father and brother, he saw those things 'which eye hath not seen,' spoke those things which 'ear hath not heard,' and uttered those things 'which have not entered into the heart of man to conceive,' 2 Cor. ii. 9. This knot needs no cutting. He that rightly understands the text will easily look through this mystery without the help of an hyperbole. His scope was to stir us up to love God; his motive to persuade is taken from the excellency of those things which God hath prepared for them who love him. That excellency is expressed in a strange manner; by intimating it cannot be expressed, no, nor so much as comprehended by any natural ability of the body or mind. Yet it is expressed in the doctrine of the gospel sufficiency. So as here, as in a glass, we may 'behold the glory of God,' and in beholding, be 'changed from glory to glory,' 2 Cor. iii. 18. What duty more necessary than to love God? What motive more effectual than the gospel? For what is the gospel but a revelation of such things as natural men could never invent? Such things, that is, so pre-

1

cious, so useful, so comfortable to us; so divine, admirable, and transcendent in themselves. Many of us are like the angel of Ephesus, 'We have lost our first love,' Rev. ii. 4; yea, as our Saviour prophesied, Matt. xxiv. 12, 'The love of many waxes cold.' One reason may be, because to see-to,[1] we reap so little fruit of our love. Were it so, that we had nothing in hand, no present pay, that we served God altogether upon trust, without so much as an earnest, yet there is something 'prepared.' Let us believe that, and our hearts cannot but be warmed. We shall then be 'fervent in spirit, serving the Lord,' Rom. xii. 11. Be we persuaded of that, 'God is not unrighteous to forget your work and labour of love, which you have showed towards his name,' Heb. vi. 10, and then we may triumphantly insult[2] with Paul, 'Who shall separate us from the love of Christ?' Rom. viii. 35. There is this difference between natural sight and spiritual. The one requires some nearness of the object, the other perceives things at greatest distance. As faith makes future things present, so it makes remote things near, and things 'prepared' to affect as if they were enjoyed. But what hath God prepared? If I could answer this, it might not only satisfy, but inebriate. 'Such as eye hath not seen,' &c. It seems to be a proverbial form of speech, whereby the rich plenty of the divine blessings and benefits which God intendeth to us in and by Christ, according to the gospel, is shadowed forth. The words are to see-to[3] as a riddle, but here is 'one of a thousand, an interpreter,' Job xxxiii. 23, at hand, to unfold them. I could say much to invite you, but that the matter itself is as a loadstone. My testimony will add little weight, yet, having some care committed to me by Mr P. N., whom this business chiefly concerned, I could do no less than let you understand here is one rich piece of spiritual workmanship, wrought by a master builder, very useful for the building up and beautifying of God's temples. The blessing of God Almighty be with it, and upon the whole Israel of God. —So prays

L. Seaman.

---

1    That is, outward appearances. —G.

2    That is, exult, boast. —G.

3    That is, sense. —G.

# THE FIRST SERMON

*But, as it is written, Eye hath not seen, nor ear heard,*
*neither have entered into the heart of man, the things*
*which God hath prepared for them that love him.*
1 Cor. ii. 9.

The holy apostle St Paul, the trumpet of the gospel, 'the vessel of election,' was ordained to be a messenger of reconciliation, and to spread the sweet savour of the gospel everywhere. And answerably to his calling, he makes way for the excellency of his embassage into the hearts of those he had to deal with. This he doth by the commendation of his function. And that he might the better prevail, he removes all objections to the contrary. There were some that would debase his office, saying that the gospel he taught—Christ crucified—was no such great matter. Therefore, in the 6th verse of this chapter, he shows that the gospel 'is wisdom, and that among them that are perfect;' among the best and ablest to judge. St Paul did not build, as the papists do now, upon the blindness of the people. But it were not popery if they did not infatuate the people. St Paul saith to this effect: We dare appeal to those that are the best, and of the best judgment, let them judge whether it be wisdom or no; the more perfect men are, the more able they are to judge of our wisdom.

It might be objected again, You see who cares for your wisdom, neither Herod, nor Pilate, nor the great men and potentates, the scribes and pharisees, great, learned men, and withal men of innocent lives, notable for carnage. Therefore, saith he, 'We speak not the wisdom of this world, or the princes of this world, that come to nought.' Do not tell its of such men's wisdom, they and their wisdom will come to nought too. We teach wisdom of things that are eternal, to make men eternal. As for the princes of the world, they and all that they know, their thoughts and all their plots and devices, perish. But 'we speak the wisdom of God in a mystery;' that is, the wisdom of God's

3

revealing, a deep wisdom, a mystery that 'God ordained before the world;' ancient wisdom, not a yesterday's knowledge, though lately discovered. The preaching of the gospel is the discovery of that wisdom that was hidden before the world was.

And to invite you, and make you more in love with it, it is a wisdom 'to your glory.' God hath a delight to show himself wise in devising a plot to glorify poor wretched man.

As for the words themselves, they are a proof of what he had said before, why none of the princes of the world knew this great mystery. If so be that the 'eye of any man hath not seen, nor the ear of any man hath heard, nor the heart of any man hath conceived,' what do you tell us of the wise men, which were not all, nay, what should I speak of men? The very angels (as we know by other places) are excluded from a full knowledge of these mysteries. Therefore it is no marvel though none of the princes of this world knew them. They are universally hidden from all natural men. This I take to be the sense of the words. They are taken out of Isaiah lxiv. 4. St Paul delights to prove things by the prophets. But here it is not so much a proof as an allusion, which we must observe to understand many such places. For Isaiah there speaks of the great things God had done for his church, such as eye had not seen, nor ear heard. And the apostle alludes to it here, and adds somewhat. This clause, 'nor hath entered into the heart of man,' is not in that place, but it is necessarily understood. For if the eye doth not see, and the ear hear, it never enters into the heart of man. For whatsoever enters into the heart of man, it must be by those passages and windows, the gates of the soul, the senses.

And whereas St Paul saith, 'for them that love him,' it is for them that 'expect him,' as in Isaiah. The sense is all one. Whosoever love God, they expect and wait for him. Where there is no expectation, there is no love.

This is the apostle's drift. If God did do such great matters for his church, as 'eye hath not seen, nor ear heard,' according to the prophet Isaiah, what shall we think he will do in the kingdom of grace here and of glory hereafter?

The words then, as we see, contain the excellency of the mysteries of the gospel, described first by the hiddenness of it to men at first.

Secondly, By the goodness of the things revealed, such as 'neither eye hath seen,' &c.

The hiddenness and excellency of the gospel in that respect is set forth by way of negation. 'Eye hath not seen, nor ear heard, nor heart conceived.' And indeed this is the way to set forth excellent divine things. God himself is set out by way of denial; by removing imperfections: he is invisible, immortal, &c. And so heaven, that is near to God, as being prepared by him, it is set out by way of denial, as St Peter saith, 'It is an inheritance immortal, undefiled,' &c., 1 Peter i. 4.

So here positive words could not be found sufficient to set out the excellency of the things that God hath prepared.

As for the knowledge of the mystery of salvation in Jesus Christ, we neither can come to it by natural invention nor by natural discipline. All the things that we know naturally, we know by one of these two ways; but divine things are known neither way.

Where could there have been any knowledge of Christ, if God had not opened his breast in the gospel, and come forth of his hidden light, and showed himself in Christ, God-man; and in publishing the gospel established an ordinance of preaching for this purpose—where had the knowledge of salvation in Christ been?

To prove this we have here a gradation. The eye sees many things, but we hear more things than we see. Yet 'neither eye hath seen nor ear heard.' Ay, but the conceits of the heart are larger than the sight of the eye or the hearing of the ear. Yet neither eye hath seen, nor ear hath heard, nor hath entered into the heart of man to conceive,' &c. The philosopher saith, there is nothing in the understanding, but it came into the senses before: and therefore it cannot enter into the heart of man, if it enter not by the eye or by the ear.

The things here spoken of be especially the graces, and comforts, and privileges to be enjoyed in this life, and the consummation and perfection of them in heaven. Christ brings peace and joy, justification and sanctification, and the like; and even in this life. The perfection of these is in heaven, where the soul and the body shall be both glorified, in a glorious place, together with glorious company; the Father, Son, and Holy Ghost, innumerable angels and just men. These are those things that 'eye hath not seen,' &c.; the beginnings here, and the perfection and consummation of them hereafter. Having thus far unfolded the words, I come to the points considerable.

*Doct. First, God hath a company of beloved children in the world, that he means a special good unto.*

The *second, God hath prepared great matters for them.*

1. If great persons prepare great things for those whom they greatly affect,[4] shall we not think that the great God will prepare great things for those that he hath affection to, and that have affection to him? If God be a friend to the elect, and they be his friends, surely he will answer friendship to the utmost. Answerable to the great love he bears his children, he hath provided great things for them.

If that be excellent that is long in preparing, then those things which belong to God's children must needs be excellent; for they were preparing even before the world was. Solomon's temple was an excellent fabric; it had long preparation, 1 Chron. xxii. 5. Ahasuerus made a feast to a hundred and twenty-seven provinces, Esther i. 1, *seq*. It was long in preparing. Great things have great preparation. Now these things that God intends his children have been preparing even from everlasting; and they are from everlasting to everlasting. They must needs be excellent. But before I dwell on any particular point, here is a question to be answered.

*Quest.* If the things that God hath prepared for his children be secret and excellent, how then come we to know them at all?

We come to know them (1.) *By divine revelation.* God must reveal them first, as it is in the next verse, 'God hath revealed them by his Spirit.'

The Spirit reveals them by way of negation, and indefinitely; as also by way of eminence. Whatsoever is excellent in the world, God borrows it to set out the excellency of the things that he hath provided for his children in grace and glory.

A feast is a comfortable thing. They are called a feast. A kingdom is a glorious thing. They are called a kingdom. Marriage is a sweet thing. They are set forth by that; by an inheritance; and adoption of children, and such like. So that all these things are taken to be shadows of those things. And indeed they are but shadows; the reality is the heavenly kingdom of grace and glory, the heavenly riches, the heavenly inheritance, the heavenly sonship. When all these things vanish and come to nothing, then comes in the true kingdom, sonship, and inheritance.

Again (2.) We know them in this world *by way of taste*. For the things of the life to come there are few of them but

---

4    That is, 'love', 'choose' — G.

God's children have some experimental taste of them in this world. God reserves not all for the life to come, but he gives a grape of Canaan in this wilderness.

(3.) Thirdly, *by arguing from the less to the greater*. If peace of conscience be so sweet here, what is eternal peace! If a little joy here be so pleasant and comfortable that it makes us forget ourselves, what will be that eternal joy there! If the delights of a kingdom be such that they fill men's hearts so full of contentment that ofttimes they know not themselves, what shall we think of that excellent kingdom! So by way of taste and relish we may rise from those petty things to those excellent things, which indeed are scarce a beam, scarce a drop of those excellencies.

If Peter and John, when they were in the mountain, were not their own men, — when they saw but a glimpse, but a little glory of Christ manifested in the mount, Matt. ix. 6, — what shall we think when there is the fulness of that glorious revelation at the right hand of God, where there is 'fulness of pleasures for ever'? Ps. xvi. 11. How shall our souls be filled at that time! Thus by way of rising from the lesser to the greater, by tasting, feeling, and by divine revelation, we may know in some measure the excellency of those things prepared for us.

Now to clear this thing more fully, know that there are three degrees of revelation.

*First, There must be a revelation of the things themselves, by word, and writing, or speech,* and the like; as we know not the mind of a man but either by speech or writing. So there must be a revelation of these things, or else the wit of angels could never have devised how to reconcile justice and mercy, by infinite wisdom, by sending a mediator to procure peace, God-man, to work our salvation. Therefore we could not know them without a revelation and discovery outward. This is the first degree, that we may call revelation by Scripture, or by the doctrine of the gospel. Who could discover those things that are merely supernatural, but God himself?

*Second, Then again, When they are revealed by the word of God, and by men that have a function to unfold the unsearchable riches of Christ by the ministry of the gospel,* yet notwithstanding they are hidden riddles still to a company of carnal men. Put case the veil be taken off from the things themselves, yet if the veil be over the soul, the understanding, will, and affections, there is no apprehension of them. Therefore there must he a second revelation, that is, by the

Spirit of God. Of necessity this must be; for even as the apostle saith in this chapter, 'None knoweth the mind of man but the spirit that is in man,' ver. 11, so none knoweth the mind of God but the Spirit of God. What is the gospel, without the Spirit of Christ to discover the mind of God to us? We know not the good meaning of God to us in particular. We know in general that such things are revealed in Scripture; but what is that to us if Christ be not our Saviour and God our Father unless we can say as St Paul saith, 'He loved me, and gave himself for me,' Gal. ii. 20. Therefore you see a necessity of revelation by the Spirit.

But this is not all that is here meant. There is,

*Thirdly, A higher discovery, and that is in heaven.* That that is revealed here is but in part; and thereupon if we believe, we believe but in part, and we love but in part. If our knowledge, which is the ground of all other graces and affections, be imperfect, all that follows must needs be imperfect also. Therefore St John saith, 'We know that we are the sons of God, but it appears not what we shall be,' 1 John iii. 2. What we shall be in heaven it doth not appear now. There must be a further revelation, and that will he hereafter, when our souls shall be united together with our bodies. And then, indeed, our eyes shall see, our ears hear, and hearts shall conceive those things that while we are here in the womb of the church we neither can see, nor hear, nor understand, more than the child in the womb of the mother can conceive the excellencies in this civil[5] life. Thus we see these truths a little more unfolded. I will now add somewhat to make use of what hath been spoken.

*Use* 1. *First* of all, therefore, for *matter of instruction.* If it be so, that the things of the gospel be such, as that without a revelation from God they could not be known, then we see that *there is no principle at all of the gospel in nature.* There is not a spark of light, or any inclination to the gospel, but it is merely above nature. For he removes here all natural ways of knowing the gospel, eye, ear, and understanding. Therefore the knowledge of it is merely supernatural. For if God had not revealed it, who could ever have devised it? And when he revealed it, to discover it by his Spirit, it is supernatural; but in heaven much more, which is the third degree I spoke of. Therefore, by the way, you may know the reason why so many heresies have sprung out of the gospel, more than out of the law and the misunderstanding of it. There are few or no

---

5    That is, 'outward life.'—G.

heresies from that, because the principles of the law are written in the heart. Men naturally know that whoredom, and adultery, and filthy living, &c., are sins. Men have not so quenched nature but that they know that those things are naught. Therefore there have been excellent law-makers among the heathens. But the gospel is a mere 'mystery' discovered out of the breast of God, without[6] all principles of nature. There are thousands of errors that are not to be reckoned, about the nature, the person, and the benefits of Christ; about justification and sanctification, and free will and grace, and such things. What a world of heresies have proud wits continually started up! This would never have been but that the gospel is a thing above nature. Therefore, when a proud wit and supernatural knowledge revealed meet together, the proud heart storms and loves to struggle, and deviseth this thing and that thing to commend itself; and hereupon comes heresies, the mingling of natural wit with divine truths. If men had had passive wits to submit to divine truths, and to work nothing out of themselves, as the spider out of her own bowels, there had not been such heresies in the church; but their hearts meeting with supernatural truths, their proud hearts mingling with it, they have devised these errors; that I note in the first place.

*Use* 2. Then again, if the things that we have in the gospel be such divine truths, above nature altogether, *then we must not stand to look for reason too much, nor trust the reason or wit of any man, but divine authority especially*. For if divine authority cease in the gospel, what were it? Nothing. The law is written in men's hearts; but we must trust divine authority in the gospel above all other portions of Scripture, and not to the wit of any man whatsoever.

The Church of Rome, that is possessed with a spirit of pride and ignorance and tyranny, they will force knowledge on them that be under them from their sole authorities. The church saith so, and we are the church; and it is not for you to know, &c., and Scriptures are so and so. But is the gospel a supernatural mystery above the capacity of any man and shall we build upon the authority of the church for these truths? Oh, no! There must be no forcing of evangelical truths from the authority or parts of any man. But these are not things that we stand in so much need of. Therefore I hasten to that which is more useful. 'Eye hath not seen, nor ear heard,' &c.

---

6   That is, 'outside of.' —G.

*Use* 3. Here then we have an use of direction *how to carry ourselves in reading and studying holy truths: especially the sacred mysteries of the gospel.* How shall we study them? We think to break into them with the engine of our wit, and to understand them, and never come to God for his Spirit. God will curse such proud attempts. 'Who knows the things of man, but the spirit of a man? and who knows the things of God, but the Spirit of God?' Therefore in studying the gospel, let us come with a spirit of faith, and a spirit of humility and meekness. There is no breaking into these things with the strength of parts. That hath been the ground of so many heresies as have been in the church. Only Christ 'hath the key of David, that shutteth, and no man openeth; and openeth, and no man shutteth,' Rev. iii. 7. He hath the key of the Scripture, and the key to open the understanding. And to press this point a little. If 'eye hath not seen, nor ear heard, nor hath entered into the heart of man to conceive, the things of the gospel,' without the revelation of the Spirit, then we must come with this mind when we come to hear the things of the gospel. Lord, without thy Holy Spirit they are all as a clasped book; they are hidden mysteries to me, though they be revealed in the gospel. If my heart be shut to them, they are all hidden to me.

We see men of excellent parts are enemies to that they teach themselves, opposing the power of the gospel. Whence is all this? Because they think only the opening of these things makes them divines, whereas without the Holy Ghost sanctifying and altering the heart in some measure to taste and relish these things, that as they are divine in themselves, so to have somewhat divine in the heart to taste these things, it is impossible but that the heart should rise against them; and so it doth. For when it comes to particulars, you must deny yourself in this honour, in this pleasure, and commodity; now you must venture the displeasure of man for this and that truth. The heart riseth in scorn and loathing of divine truth. When it comes to particulars they know nothing as they should. For when is truth known, but when in particulars we stand for it; and will neither betray it nor do anything that doth not benefit[7] a Christian? If we have not the Spirit of God to relish truths in particular, they will do us no good. And except the Spirit sanctify the heart of man first by these truths, the truth will never be understood by the proud natural

---

7   Qu. 'befit'? — ED.

heart of man.

Therefore the course that God takes with his children is this. Those that he means to save, he first inspires into their hearts some desire to come to hear and attend upon the means of salvation, to understand the gospel; and then under the means of salvation he shines into the understanding by a heavenly light, and inspires into the will and affections some heavenly inclination to this truth of the gospel, to justification, sanctification, self-denial, and the like, and works a new life; and new senses, and upon them, wrought under the means, comes the soul to relish, and to understand these mysteries; and then the ears and the eyes are open to see these things, and never before. A holy man, that hath his heart subdued by the Spirit of God in the use of the means, oh he relisheth the point of forgiveness of sins; he relisheth the point of sanctification; he studies it daily more and more, and nearer communion with God; he relisheth peace of conscience and joy in the Holy Ghost; they are sweet things, and all the duties of Christianity, because he makes it his main business to adorn his profession; and to live here, so as he may live for ever hereafter. And this must be of necessity; for mark out of the text: if the natural eye and ear and heart can never see nor hear, nor conceive the things of God, must there not be a supernatural ear and eye and heart put into the soul? Must not the heart and all be new-moulded again? If the former frame be not sufficient for these things, of necessity it must be so.

*Use* 4. From hence learn *to arm yourselves against all scandals*.[8] When ye see men of all parts and account, and such there may be, men of deep apprehensions and understanding in the Scripture for the matter of notion, and for the language of the Scripture exquisite, and yet to be proud, malicious, haters of sanctity, next to devils, none greater, consider what is the reason. Either they have proud spirits that despise and neglect the means of salvation altogether; or if they do come, they come as judges; they will not submit their proud hearts to the sweet motions of the Spirit. Stumble not at it, if such men be both enemies to that they teach themselves, and those that practise it. The reason is, because their proud hearts were never subdued by the Spirit to understand the things they speak of. For such a teacher understands supernatural things by a natural light, and by human reason; that is, to talk, and

---

8    That is, 'Stumbling-blocks.'—G.

discourse, &e., but he sees not supernatural things by a supernatural light, divine things by a divine light. Therefore a poor soul that hears the things published by him, understands them better by the help of the Spirit than he that speaks them; better indeed for his use and comfort. As we see, there are some that can measure land exactly; but the man that owneth the land measured, he knows the use of the ground and delights in it as his own. The other can tell, here is so much ground, &c. So some divines, they can tell there are such points, and so they are raised; and they can be exquisite in this; but what profit have they by it?

The poor soul that hears these things, by the help of the Spirit he can say, These are mine, as the man for whom the ground is measured. As it is with those that come to a feast, the physician comes and says, This is wholesome and good, and this is good for this and that, but eats nothing. Others that know not these things, they eat the meat, and are nourished in the mean time. So when such men discourse of this and that, a poor man that hath the Spirit, he relisheth these things as his own. The other goes away, only discourseth as a philosopher of the meat, and eats nothing.

And therefore when thou read and hear these things, content not yourselves with the first degree of revelation. No; that is not enough. When you have done that, desire of God to join his Spirit, to give you spiritual eyes and hearts, that you may close with divine truths, and be divine as the truths are; that there may be a consent of the heart with the truth. Then the word of God will be sweet indeed.

*Use* 5. Again, here we see this divine truth, *that a man when he hath the Spirit of God knows things otherwise than he did know them before, though he did not know them by outward revelation of hearing and reading, &c.* And he believes them otherwise than he did before; he sees them by a new light. It is not the same knowledge that an unregenerate man hath with that he hath after, when God works upon his heart, 1 Cor. ii. 14, 15; for then it is a divine supernatural knowledge. And it is not the same faith and belief. The Spirit of God raiseth a man up in a degree of creatures above other men, as other men are above beasts; he gives new eyes, new ears, and a new heart; he moulds him anew every way. Therefore you have good men sometimes wonder at themselves, when God hath touched their hearts, that they have had such shallow conceits of this and that truth before. Now they see that they were in the dark, that they were in a damp before, that they conceived things to be so and so, and thought themselves somebody. But when God opens their eyes, and takes away the scales, and lets them see things in their proper light, heavenly things by a heavenly light, and with a heavenly eye, they wonder at their former foolishness in divinity, especially so far as concerns the gospel. For there is more in the Scripture than pure supernatural divinity; there are many other arts in the Scripture.

The gospel, I say, is a knowledge, not of natural men, or great wits, but of holy sanctified men. Therefore we must not think that these things may be known by nature, &c. It is a sacred knowledge, so much as will bring us to heaven; it is a knowledge of holy men, that have their hearts brought to love and taste, and relish that they know. Therefore it is no wonder, though a company of men of great parts live naughtily. They are no true divines, because they have no true knowledge. The devil is no divine, nor a wicked man properly. Though he can discourse of such things, yet he is not properly a divine; because he knows not things by a divine light, or heavenly things by a heavenly light. The knowledge of the gospel, it is a knowledge of sanctified, holy men. But to come nearer to our practice.

*Use.* 6. If eye hath not seen, nor ear heard, nor hath entered into the heart of man to conceive those things that God hath prepared for his, then *let us make this the rule of our esteem of anything that is good, or anything that is ill; make it a rule of valuation.* The apostle here, you see, hath a rank of things above the sight of the eye, or the hearing of the ear, or the conceiving of the heart of man. If there be such a rank of things above this, then the greatest ills are those that eye hath not seen, nor ear heard, nor hath entered into the heart of man; and indeed they are so. We grieve at the ague, and at the stone, and at the gout; they are grievous things indeed. Oh, but what be these things that we feel and see, to those in another world, that we cannot apprehend for the greatness of them! The torments of hell, we cannot conceive and understand them here; for it is indeed to be in hell itself to conceive what hell is. And therefore when God enlargeth men's spirits to see them, they make away themselves. And so for the greatest good. These goods here, this outward glory, we can see through it. Christ could see through all the glory in the world that the devil showed him, Matt. iv. 8. And these are things that we can hear of, and hear the utmost that can be spoken of them. Therefore surely they are not the greatest good. There are more excellent things than they. Because the eye sees them, the ear hears of them, and the understanding can conceive of them. But there be things that the eye hath not seen, nor ear heard, nor the soul conceived; and these be the joys of heaven. And thereupon, to descend to practice, if this be a rule to value things that the best things are transcendent, beyond sense and comprehension, then shall I for those things that I can see, and can hear, and feel, and understand, shall I lose those excellent good things, that 'neither eye hath seen nor ear heard,' &c.? Is not this desperate folly, to venture the loss of the best things, of the most transcendent things, that are above the capacity of the greatest reaches of the world? Shall I lose all for petty poor things that are within my own reach and compass?

How foolish, therefore, are those that are given to pleasures! They feel the pleasure indeed, but the sting comes after. They delight in those ill things that they can hear, and hear all that can be spoken of them, and never think of the excellent things that the eye hath not seen, nor ear heard, &c.

Let this make us in love with divine truths in the Scripture, with the gospel, that part of the Scripture that promiseth salvation by Christ, and all the graces and privileges of Christianity. They are above our reach. We study other things. We can reach them. We can reach the mysteries of the law by long study, and the mysteries of physic, and to the mysteries of trades by understanding, and when men have done all they may be fools in the main—Solomon's fools. They may do all these things, and be wise for particular things, by particular reaches of that which eye hath seen, and ear heard, &c.; and then for the best things that are above the capacity of men, they may die empty of all, and go to the place of the damned. To be wise to salvation is the best wisdom.

What a pitiful case is this, that God should give us our understandings for better things than we can see or hear in this world, yet we employ them in things of the world wholly. Let us not do as some shallow, proud heads, that regard not divine things. The holy Scriptures they will not vouchsafe to read once a-day, perhaps not once a-week; nay, some scarce have a Bible in their studies. For shame; shall we be so atheistical, when God hath provided such excellent things contained in this book of God, the Testament? Shall we slight these excellent things for knowledge that shall perish with us as St Paul saith before the text? The knowledge of all other things is perishing, knowledge of perishing men. Learn on earth that that will abide in heaven, saith St Austin. If we be wise, let us know those things on earth, that the comfort of them may abide with us in heaven. Therefore let us be stirred up to value the Scriptures, the mysteries of salvation in the gospel; they are things that 'eye hath not seen, nor ear heard,' &c. Nay, I say more, that little that we have here, by hearing truths unfolded, whereby the Spirit of God slides into our hearts, and works with them. There is that peace that a man hath in his heart, in the unfolding of the point of justification or adoption, or any divine comfort, that it breeds such inward peace and joy as is unspeakable and glorious. All that we have in the world is not worth those little beginnings that are wrought by the hearing of the word of God here. If the first fruits here be joy ofttimes 'unspeakable and glorious,' 1 Peter i. 8, if the first fruits be 'peace that passeth understanding,' Phil. iv. 7, what will the consummation and perfection of these things be at that day?

Again, here you see a ground of the wonderful patience of the martyrs. You wonder that they would suffer their bodies to be torn, and have their souls severed so violently from their bodies. Alas![9] cease to wonder; when they had a sense wrought in them by the Spirit of God of the things that eye hath not seen nor ear heard. If a man should have asked them why they would suffer their bodies to be misused thus, when they might have redeemed all this with a little quiet? Oh, they would have answered presently, as some of them have done: We suffer these things in our bodies and in our senses, for those that are above our senses; we know there are things laid up for us that eye hath not seen, nor ear heard, &c. What do you tell us of this torment and that torment? We shall have more glory in heaven than we can have misery here. For we can see this, and there is an end of it; but we shall have joy that eye hath not seen, nor ear heard, &c. As St Paul most divinely, in divers places in Rom. viii. 18, the things that we suffer here are not 'worthy of the glory that shall be revealed.' Therefore let us not wonder so much at their patience as to lay up this ground of patience against an evil day when we may be drawn to seal the truth with our blood. By the way learn what popery is. They think to merit by their doings,

---

9    Another example of Sibbe's unusual use of 'alas.' — G.

but especially by their sufferings, though they be ill doers, and suffer for their demerits; this is their glory. Shall those stained good works (put case they were good works, they be defiled, and stained, and as menstruous cloths, as it is, Isa. xxx. 22), shall they merit the glory to be revealed, that is so great that eye hath not seen? &c. What proportion is there? In merit there must be a proportion between the deed done and the glory. What proportion is there between stained imperfect defiled works, and the glory to be revealed? Should not our lives be almost angelical? 'What manner of men should we be in all holy conversation,' 2 Pet. iii. 11, considering what things are laid up in heaven, and we have the first fruits of them here? Can men be too holy and exact in their lives, that look for things 'that eye hath not seen, nor ear heard?' &c.

I wonder at the stupidity and hellish pride and malice of men's hearts, that think any man can be too exact in the main duties of Christianity, in the expression of their love to God, in the obedience of their lives; in abstinence from the filthiness of the world, and the like. Can a man that looks for these excellent transcendent things be too careful of his life? I beseech you yourselves be judges.

# THE SECOND SERMON

*As it is written, Eye hath not seen, nor ear heard, &c.*
1 Cor. ii. 9.

The apostle sets out the gospel here with all the commendations that any skill in the world can be commended by. From the author of it, 'God.' From the depth of it, it is 'wisdom;' in a mystery, 'hidden wisdom.' From the antiquity of it, 'it was ordained before the world was.' From the benefit and use of it, 'for our glory.' *God is content his wisdom should be honoured in glorifying us, such is his love.* And then when it was revealed, that none of the 'princes of the world' (he means not only commanding potentates, but, he being a scholar himself, esteemed philosophers, Pharisees, and learned men to be princes, because the excellency of a man is in the refined part of man, his soul), none of these princes of the world, for all their skill and knowledge, knew this.

In this verse he shows the reason why 'eye hath not seen, nor ear heard,' &c. He removes knowledge, by removing the way and means of knowledge. The means of knowledge in this world is by the passage and entrance of the senses. Now, this heavenly mystery of the gospel, it is such a knowledge as doth not enter into the soul by the senses.

The points we propounded were these: 1. *That God hath a people in the world, whom he favours in a special manner.*

Then, secondly, *for these that he accounts his friends, he hath prepared great matters.* Kings prepare great matters for those they mean to advance; what shall we think then God will do for his friends?

Now, these things prepared, they are great matters indeed; for, in the third place, they are such as *eye hath not seen, nor ear heard, &c.*

And then, in the fourth place, *the disposition and qualification of those for whom God hath prepared such great matters.* It is for those 'that love him;' not for his enemies, or for all men indifferently, but for those that love him.

Of the first and second I spoke in the former; and I will not now stand to speak of them, but enlarge myself in the two last.

*The things that God hath prepared for them that love him, are such excellent things as neither eye hath seen, nor ear heard, &c.* He means the natural eye, and ear, and understanding, or heart of man.

There are three degrees of discovery of heavenly things:

First, In the *doctrine of them*; and so they are hid to them that are out of the church.

And then, secondly, in *the spiritual meaning of them*; and so they are hid to carnal men in the church.

And then, thirdly, in regard of *the full comprehension of them*, as they are indeed; and so they are reserved for heaven. We have but a little glimpse of them, a little light into them in this world. Now, in this place is meant the things that are discovered in the gospel, especially as they are apprehended by the Spirit, together with the consummation of them in heaven. For they differ only in degree, the discovery of the heavenly things in the gospel here; the privileges, and graces, and comforts of God's children, and the consummation of them in heaven. And we may reason from the lesser to the greater, if so be that a natural man—though he have natural eyes, and ears, and wits about him—cannot conceive the hidden mysteries of the gospel spiritually with application; much more unable is he, and much less can he conceive, those things of a better life. Now the things of the gospel, the privileges, the graces, and comforts which Christ, the spring and head of them all, in whom all are, and whence we have all, cannot be comprehended by a natural man. He can discourse of them as far as his natural wit conceives them, but not understand heavenly things in their own light as heavenly things, as the things of the gospel. They can talk of repentance—that we commonly speak of, which is a mystery—but notwithstanding who knows repentance by the light proper to it, but he that by the Spirit of God hath sin discovered to him in its own colours! He knows what it is to grieve for sin.

The sick man knows what it is to be sick. The physician knows it by definition, by books, and so he can enlarge it; but if he is not sick, the sick patient will speak to better purpose. So there is a mystery in the common things of the gospel, repentance and grief for sin. A holy man feels it another matter, because he feels sin discovered by the Spirit of God. And so in faith, in the love of God, and every grace of the gospel is a mystery. If one come to the Schoolmen, they will tell you of faith, and dispute learnedly of it, and deduce this from that; but when he comes to be in extremity, when the terrors of the Lord are upon him, when he comes to use it, he is a mere stranger to it; to cast himself, being a sinful creature, into the arms of God's mercy, he cannot do it without a further light of the Spirit discovering the hidden love of God to him in particular; and so for other graces. Therefore they do but speak of these things—men that are unsanctified—as a blind man doth of colours. They inwardly scorn the truth they speak of; and those to whom they speak, if by the power of God's Spirit they come to profit by the things they teach, if themselves be carnal, they hate them. A carnal man believes not a whit of what he saith; he hath only a common light for the good of others, a common illumination to understand and discover things, and a doctrinal gift to unfold things for others, and not for themselves. For themselves they scorn them in their hearts, and in their lives and conversations, and they will speak as much when it comes to self-denial in preferment, in pleasures, in anything that is gainful. Tush! tell him what he hath taught, or what he knows out of the book of God, he cares not, he knows them only by a common light; but for a particular heavenly light with application and taste to himself, springing from an alteration by the Spirit, he never knows them so. Therefore content not thyself with a common light, for together with our understanding God alters the taste of the whole soul; he gives a new eye, a new ear, to see and hear to purpose, and a new heart to conceive things in another manner than he did before.

But you will ask, How can a godly man know them at all, seeing 'eye hath not seen, nor ear heard,' &c.?

I answer, *first*, the things of another life, as we see here, *are known by negation,* as God is, by way of removing imperfections. The natural eye sees them not, nor the natural ear hears them not, &c. No; nor the spiritual eye nor ear in a full measure. So things transcendent, that are above the reach of man, are described in the Scriptures by the way of denial, which is one good way of knowledge.

That 'ye may know the love of God that is above knowledge,' saith the apostle, Eph. iii. 19; that ye may know it more and more. But it is above all knowledge in regard of the perfection of it. As a man may see the sea, but he cannot comprehend the sea. He may he much delighted in seeing the sea, but he sees neither the bottom nor the banks; he cannot comprehend such a vast body. He may see the heavens, but he cannot comprehend them. So a man may know the things when they are revealed, but he cannot comprehend them; apprehension is one thing, and comprehension is another. There may he apprehension in a poor degree, suitable to the capacity of the soul here; but, alas! it is far from the comprehension that we shall have in heaven. That is one way of knowing them, by way of negation and denial of imperfections to them.

And then, *secondly*, they are known, as we call it, by way of *eminence*; that is, by comparing them with other things, and preferring them before all other excellencies whatsoever; as we may see the sun in water by resemblance. For God borrows from nature terms to set out grace and glory, because God will speak in our language. For they are called a 'kingdom' and a 'feast,' and a 'crown' by way of comparison. Shallow men think there is a great deal in a kingdom; and indeed so there is, if there were no other. There is great matters in a 'crown,' in 'the feasts' of kings, and the like. But alas! these are shadows; and there is no rhetoric or amplification in this, to say they be shadows. A shadow is as much in proportion to the body as these are to eternal good things. The true reality of things are in the things of another world, for eternity. If we talk of a kingdom, let us talk of that in heaven; if of a crown, of that wherewith the saints are crowned in heaven. If we talk of riches, they are those that make a man eternally rich; that he shall carry with him when he goes out of the world. What riches are those that a man shall outlive, and die a beggar, and not have a drop to comfort him, as we see Dives in hell had not? Luke xvi. 19, *seq.* Here are riches indeed. So if we talk of beauty, it is the image of God that sets a beauty on the soul, that makes a man lovely in the eye of God. True beauty is to be like God. And to be born anew to that glorious condition is the birth and inheritance. All these poor things are but acting a part upon a stage for a while, as the proudest creature of all that is invested in them will judge ere long; none better judges than they. This is one way of knowing the things of the gospel, by naming of them in our own language. As if a man go into a foreign country, he must learn that language, or else hold his peace: so God is forced to speak in our own language, to tell us of glory and happiness to come, under the name of crowns and kingdoms, and riches here. If God should set them out in their own lustre, we could not conceive of them.

But, *thirdly*, the most comfortable way whereby God's people know the things of heaven, and of the life to come, *is in regard of some taste*; for there is nothing in heaven but God's children have a taste of it before they come there in some measure. They have a taste of the communion that is in heaven, in the communion they have on earth: they have a taste of that eternal Sabbath, by some relish they have of holy exercises in these Christian Sabbaths. A Christian is as much in heaven as he can be, when he sanctifies the holy Sabbath, speaking to God in the congregation by prayer, and hearing God speak to him in the preaching of the word. That peace that we shall have in heaven, which is a peace uninterrupted, without any disturbance, it is understood by that sweet peace of conscience here 'that passeth all understanding,' Eph. iii. 19. We may know, therefore, what the sight of Christ face to face will be, by the sight we have of Christ now in the word and promises. If it so transform and affect us, that sight that we have by knowledge and faith here, what will those sights do? So that by a grape we may know what Canaan is: as the spies, they brought of the grapes of Canaan into the desert. We may know by this little taste what these excellent things are.

The *fourth* way is by *authority and discovery*. St Paul was rapt up in[to] the third heaven; he saith, they were such things that he saw, that could not be spoken of, strange things, 2 Cor. xii. 4. And Christ tells us of a kingdom. Christ knew what they were. And the word tells us what they are. Our faith looks to the authority of the word, if we had not the first fruits, nor any other discovery. God that hath prepared them, he saith so in his word, and we must rest in his authority. And there are some that have been in heaven. Christ our blessed Saviour, that hath taken into a perpetual union the manhood with the second person, which he hath knit unto it, he knows what is there; and by this means we come to have some kind of knowledge of the things to come.

*Fifthly*, Again, *by a kind of reasoning likewise from the lesser to the greater*, we may come to know not only the things, but the greatness of them. As, is there not comfort now in a little glimpse, when God shines upon a Christian's soul, when he is as it were in heaven? Is there such contentment in holy company here, what shall there be in heaven? Is there such contentment in the delights of this world, that are the delights of our pilgrimage? (They are no better; our houses are houses of pilgrimage; our contentments are contentments of passengers.) If the way, the gallery that leads to heaven, be so spread with comforts, what be those that are reserved in another world! A man may know by raising his soul from the lesser to the greater. And if the things that God hath provided in common for his enemies as well as his friends (as all the comforts of this world, all the delicacies and all the objects of the senses, they are comforts that are common to the enemies of God, as well as his friends): if these things be so excellent, that men venture their souls for them, and lose all to be drowned in these things, Oh what peculiar things are they that God hath reserved for his own children, for those that love him, when those that are common with his enemies are so glorious and excellent! These kind of ways we may come to know them by the help of the Spirit.

Those unmixed joys, those pure joys, that are full of themselves, and have no tincture in heaven, are understood by those joys we feel on earth; the joy of the Holy Ghost, which is after conflict with temptations, or after afflictions, or after hearing and meditating on good things. The heavenly joys that flow into the soul, they give us a taste of that full joy that we shall have at the right hand of God for evermore. That comfort that we shall have in heaven, in the presence of God, and of Christ, and his holy angels, is understood in some little way by the comfortable presence of God to the soul of a Christian, when he finds the Spirit of God raising him, and cheering him up, and witnessing his presence; as ofttimes, to the comfort of God's people, the Holy Ghost witnesseth a presence, that now the soul can say, God is present with me, he smiles on me, and strengtheneth me, and leads me along. This comfortable way God's children have to understand the things of heaven, by the first fruits they have here. For God is so far in love with his children here on earth, and so tender over them, that he purposes not to reserve all for another world, but gives them some taste beforehand, to make them better in love with the things there, and better to bear the troubles of this world. But alas! what is it to that that they shall know? as it is 1 John iii. 2, 'Now we are the sons of God, but it appears not what we shall be.' That shall be so great in comparison of that we are, that it is said not to appear at all. It appears in the first fruits in a little beginnings; but alas! what is that to that glory that shall be! 'Our life is hid with Christ in God,' Col. iii. 3. It is hid. There is no man knows it in regard of the full manifestation; because here it is covered with so many infirmities, and afflictions, and so many scorns of the world are cast upon the beauty of a Christian life; it is hid in our head Christ. It is not altogether hid, for there is a life that comes from the root, from the head Christ to the members, that quickens them; but in regard of the glory that shall be, it is a hidden life.

*Reasons*. Let us consider the reasons why God will have it thus, to make it clear, before I go further. We must be modest in reasons when we speak of God's counsels and courses. I will only name them to open our understandings a little.

*1st Reason*. (*First*.) *It is enough that God will have it so.* A modest Christian will be satisfied with that, that God will have a difference between heaven and earth. God's dispensation may satisfy them.

(*Second*.) *God will have a difference between the warring church and the triumphing church.*

This life is a life of faith, and not of sight. We walk and live by faith. Why? Partly to try the truth of our faith, and partly for the glory of God, that he hath such servants in the world here that will depend upon him, upon terms of faith, upon his bare word; that can say, There are such things reserved in heaven for me, I have enough. What a glory is it to God that he hath those that will trust him upon his bare word! It were no commendation for a Christian to live here in a beautiful, glorious manner, if he should see all and live by sight. If he should see hell open, and the terrors there, for him then to abstain from sin, what glory were it! The sight would force abstinence. If we should see heaven open, and the joys of it present, it were no thanks to be a good man, for sight would force it.

*2nd Reason*. The second reason is this, *that God will have a known difference between hypocrites and the true children of God.* If heaven were upon earth, and nothing reserved in faith and in promise, every one would he a Christian. But now the greatest things being laid up in promises, we must exercise our faith to wait for them. Now, there are none that will honour God in his word but the true Christian. That there are such excellent things reserved in another world, in comparison of which all these are base, there is none but a true Christian that will honour God upon his word, that will venture the loss of these things here for them in heaven, that will not lose those things that they have in reversion and promise for the present delights of sin for a season! Whereas the common sort, they hear say of a heaven, and happiness, and a day of judgment, &c. But in the mean time they will not deny their base pleasures and their rebellious dispositions, they will cross themselves in nothing. Do we think that God hath prepared heaven for such wretches as these? Oh let us never think of it! God therefore hath reserved the best excellencies for the time to come, in promises and in his word, if we have grace to depend upon his word, and in the mean time go on and cross our corruptions. It is an excellent condition to be so. It shows the difference that God will have between us and other men.

*3rd Reason.* Again, *thirdly, our vessels could not contain it.* We are incapable; our brain is not strong enough for these things. As weak brains cannot digest hot liquors, so we cannot digest a large revelation of these things. As we see St Peter was not himself in the transfiguration; he forgot himself, and was spiritually drunk with joy, with that he saw in the mount. He wot[10] not what he said, as the scripture saith, when he said, 'Master, let us make three tabernacles,' &c., Mark ix. 5. Nay, St Paul himself, the great apostle, when he saw things in heaven above expression, that could not nor might not be uttered, could not digest them, 2 Cor. xii. 4. They were so great, that if he had not had somewhat to weigh him down, to balance him, he had been overturned with pride. Therefore there was a 'prick in the flesh' sent to Paul himself, to humble him, 2 Cor. xii. 7. Are we greater than Paul and Peter, the great apostles of the Jews and Gentiles; when these grand apostles could not contain themselves? When they see these heavenly things, and but a glimpse of them, the one did not know what he said, and the other was humbled, by way of prevention, with a prick in the flesh; and shall we think to conceive of these things? No! we cannot; for that is to be in heaven before our time. These and the like reasons we may have to satisfy us in this, why we cannot conceive of the things to come as they are in their proper nature. God saith to Moses, when Moses would have a fairer manifes-

---

10 Knew.

tation of God, 'No man can see me and live,' Exod. xxxiii.
20. If we would see God as he is, we must die. If we would
see heaven, and the joys of it as it is, we must die first. No
man can see the things that the apostle here speaks of, in
their proper light and excellency, but he must die first.

They are not proportionable to our condition here. For
God hath resolved that this life shall be a life of imperfec-
tion, and that shall be a perfect estate of perfect glory. Alas!
our capacities now are not capable, our affections will not
contain those excellent things. Therefore God trains us
up by little and little to the full fruition and enjoying of
it. Thus we see how we come to have some knowledge of
them, and why we have not a full knowledge of them here.

*Use* 1. Well, to leave this and go on. If this be so, *then
let us oft think of these things.*

The life of a Christian is wondrously ruled in this
world by the consideration and meditation of the life of
another world. Nothing more steers the life of a Christian
here than the consideration of the life hereafter; not only
by way of comfort, that the consideration of immortal
life and glory is the comfort of this mortal base life, but
likewise by way of disposition and framing a man to all
courses that are good. There is no grace of the Spirit, in a
manner, but it is set on work by the consideration of the
estate that is to come; no, not one.

What is the work of faith? 'It is the evidence of things
not seen,' Heb. xi. 1. It sets the things of another world
present before the eye of the soul, and in that respect it
is victorious. It conquers the world, because it sets a better world in the eye. Where were the exercise of faith, if
it were not for hope of such an estate which feeds faith?
The excellency of faith is, that it is about things not seen.
It makes things that are not seen to be seen; it hath a kind
of omnipotent power; it gives a being to things that have
none, but in the promise of the speaker.

And for hope, the very nature of hope is to expect
those things that faith believes. Were it not for the joys of
heaven, where were hope? It is the helmet of the soul, to
keep it from blows and temptations. It is the anchor of the
soul, that being cast within the veil into heaven, stays the
soul in all the waves and troubles in this world. The consideration of the things to come exerciseth this grace of
hope. We look within the veil, and cast anchor there upward, and not downward; and there we stay ourselves in
all combustions and confusions by the exercise of hope,

Heb. vi. 19.

And where were patience? If it were not for a better estate in another world, a Christian 'of all men were most miserable,' 1 Cor. xv. 19. Who would endure anything for Christ, if it were not for a better estate afterwards?

And so for sobriety. What forceth a moderate use of all things here? The consideration of future judgment, that made even Felix to tremble, Acts xxiv. 25. The consideration of the estate to come, causes that we surfeit not with the cares of the world and excess, but do all that may make way for such a glorious consideration.

What enforceth the keeping of a good conscience in all things? St Paul looked to the resurrection of the just and of the unjust; and this made him exercise himself to keep a good conscience.

And so purity and holiness, that we take heed of all defilements in the world, that we be not 'led away with the error of the wicked,' 2 Peter iii. 17; but 'keep ourselves unspotted,' James i. 27. What forceth this but the consideration of a glorious condition in another world! 'He that hath this hope purgeth himself,' 1 John iii. 3. There is a purgative power in hope; a cleansing efficacy, that a man cannot hope for this excellent condition, but it will frame and fit the soul for that condition. Can a man hope to appear before a great person, and not fit himself in his deportment and attire beforehand, to please the person before whom he appears? So whosoever hopes to appear before Christ and God, of necessity that hope will force him to purge himself. Let us not stand to search curiously into particulars, what the glory of the soul or of the body shall be (the apostle discovers it in general, we shall be conformed to Christ our head in soul and body'), but rather study how to make good use of them; for therefore they are revealed beforehand in general.

*Use* 2. And withal *to humble ourselves, and to say with the psalmist,* 'Lord, what is man, that thou so far considerest him?' Ps. viii. 4; sinful man, that hath lost his first condition, and hath betrayed himself to thine and his enemy; to advance him to that estate, 'that neither eye hath seen, nor ear heard,' &c. This consideration will make us base in our own eyes.

Shall not we presently disdain any proud conceits? Shall we talk of merit? What can come from a creature that shall deserve things that 'eye hath not seen nor ear heard;' that such proud conceits should enter into the heart of man? Surely grace never entered into that man's heart, that hath such a conceit to entertain merit. Shall a man think by a penny to merit a thousand pounds; by a little performance to merit things that are above the conceit of men and angels? But a word is enough that way.

*Use* 3. And *with humiliation, take that which always goes with humiliation, thankfulness, even beforehand.* When the apostle St Peter thought of the 'inheritance immortal and undefiled,' &c., he begins, 'Blessed be God, the Father of our Lord Jesus Christ,' &c., 1 Peter i. 3, 4. He could not think of these things without thankfulness to God. For we should begin the life of heaven upon earth, as much as may be; and what is that but a blessing and praising of God? Now we cannot more effectually and feelingly praise God, than by the consideration of what great things are reserved for us; for faith sets them before the soul as present, as invested into them. Now if we were in heaven already, we should praise God, and do nothing else. Therefore faith making them sure to the soul, as if we had them, sets the soul on work to praise God, as in Eph. i. 3, and in 1 Peter i. 3. St Peter and Paul, they could never have enough of this. Thus we should do, and cheer and joy our hearts in the consideration of these things in all conflicts and desolations. We little think of those things, and that is our fault. We are like little children that are born to great matters, notwithstanding not knowing of them, they carry not themselves answerable to their hopes. But the more the children grow into years, the more they grow in spirit and conceits,[11] and carriage fitting the estates they hope for.

So it is with Christians at the first; when they are weak they are troubled with this temptation and with that, with this loss and with that cross; but when a Christian grows to a full stature in Christ, every petty cross doth not cast him down. He thinks, What! shall I be dejected with this loss, that have heaven reserved for me? Shall I be cast down with this cross, that have things that 'eye hath not seen nor ear heard,' &c., prepared for me? He will not. He makes use of his faith to fetch comfort from these things that are reserved for him, that are inexpressible and inconceivable.

*Use* 4. And *let us comfort ourselves in all the slightings of the world.* A man that hath great hopes in his own country, if he be slighted abroad, he thinks with himself, I have other matters reserved elsewhere, and I shall have another

---

11 That is, 'conceptions.'—G.

manner of respect when I come home. The world it knows not God, nor Christ, nor us. Shall not we be content to go up and down as unknown men here, when God the Father and Christ our Saviour are unknown? There are better things reserved at home for us. Therefore let us digest all the slightings and abusage of carnal men. And let us not envy them their condition that is but for term of life, use it as well as they will; that hath a date that will be out we know not how soon. Alas! all their happiness it is but a measured happiness; it is within their understandings; their eyes can see it and their ears can hear it, and when they can neither see nor conceive more in this world, then there is an end of all their sensible[12] happiness. Shall we envy, when they shall shortly be turned out naked out of this world to the place of torment? We should present them to us as objects of pity, even the greatest men in the world, if we see by their carriage they be void of grace; but not envy any condition in this world. But what affection is due and suiting to the estate of a Christian? If we would have the true affection, it is admiration and wonderment. What is wonderment? It is the state and disposition of the soul toward things that are new and rare and strange; that we can give no reason of, that are beyond our reach. For wise men wonder not, because they see a reason, they can compass things. But a Christian cannot but wonder, because the things prepared are above his reach. Yea, when he is in heaven, he shall not be able to conceive the glory of it. He shall enter into it; it shall be above him; he shall have more joy and peace than he can comprehend. The joy that he hath there it is beyond his ability and capacity, beyond his power; he shall not be able to compass all. It shall be a matter of wonder even in heaven itself, much more should it be here below. Therefore the holy apostles, when they speak in the Scriptures of these things, it is with terms of admiration and wonderment, 'joy unspeakable and glorious,' 1 Peter i. 8, and 'peace that passeth understanding,' Philip. iv. 7; and when they speak of our deliverance out of the state of darkness into the state of grace, they call it a being 'brought out of darkness into his marvellous light,' 1 Peter ii. 9. And so 'God loved the world,' he cannot express how, John iii. 16. 'Behold what love hath the Father showed us, that we should be called the sons of God,' 1 John iii. 1. To be called, and to be, is all one with God; both beyond expression.

---

12  That is, 'sentient,' = sense-derived—G.

*Use* 5. Again, if this be so that God hath provided such things as neither 'eye hath seen nor ear hath heard,' &c, *beg of God first the Spirit of grace to conceive of them as the Scripture reveals them, and then beg of God a further degree of revelation*, that he would more and more reveal to us by his Spirit those excellent things. For the soul is never in a better frame than when it is lift up above earthly things. When shall a man use the world as though he used it not? When he goes about his business in a commanding manner, as seeing all things under him; when he is raised up to conceive the things that are reserved for him above the world. That keeps a man from being drowned in the world. What makes men drowned in the world to be earthworms? They think of no other heaven but this; they have no other thing in their eye. Now by the Spirit discovering these things to them that have weaned souls, it makes them go about the things of the world in another manner. They will do them, and do them exactly, with conscience and care, considering that they must give an account of all; but they will do them with reserved affections to better things. Therefore let us oft think of this, and labour to have a spirit of faith to believe them that they are so, that there are such great things; and then upon believing, the meditation of such excellent things will keep the soul in such a frame as it will be fit for anything without defiling of itself. A man that hath first faith that these things are so, and then that hath faith exorcised to think and meditate what these things are, he may be turned loose to any temptation whatsoever. For first of all, if there be any solicitation to any base sin, what will he think? Shall I for the pleasures of sin for a season, if not lose the joys of heaven and happiness that 'eye hath not seen,' &c., yet surely I shall lose the comfort and assurance of them. A man cannot enjoy the comfort of heaven upon earth without self-denial and mortification. Shall I lose peace of conscience and joy in the Holy Ghost for these things? When Satan comes with any bait, let us think he comes to rob us of better than he can give. His bait is some present pleasure, or preferment, or contentment here. But what doth he take from us? That which 'eye hath not seen, nor ear heard,' &c. He gives Adam an apple, and takes away paradise. Therefore in all temptations consider not what he offers, but what we shall lose; at least the comfort of what we shall lose. We shall lose the comfort of heaven, and bring ourselves to terrors of conscience.

Religion is not so empty a thing as that we need to be beholding to the devil for any preferment, or riches, or contentment, or pleasure. Hath God set up a profession of religion, and do we think that we must be beholding to his, and our enemy, for any base contentments? No. It is a disparagement to our religion, to our profession and calling, and to our Lord and Master we serve, to think that he will not provide richly for his. You see here he hath prepared things that 'eye hath not seen,' &c.

And by this likewise we may judge of the difference of excellencies; the difference of degrees of excellencies may be fetched from hence. The things that the eye can see they may be excellent good things, but if the eye can see them there is no great matters in them. The thing that the ear hears by reports are more than the eye sees. We may hear much that we never saw, yet if we can hear them and conceive of them upon the hearing, they are no great matters, for the soul is larger than they. We conceive more than we can hear; the conceit is beyond sight and hearing. If we can conceive the compass and latitude of anything, it is no great matter, for it is within the reach, and model, and apprehension of man's brain; it is no wondrous matter. Ay, but then the things that are most excellent of all they are above sight and beholding and hearing and conceit, that the soul cannot wholly compass and reach them. Those are the excellent things of all. The rule of excellency is to know what we can conceive, and what is beyond our comprehension. The wit of man can conceive all things under the heavens. All the knowledge we have comes within the brain of man; the government of states and the like. Oh but the things that God hath provided for his never came wholly within the brain of man, and therefore they are the most excellent!

And so by way of contraries for ills; what are the greatest ills? Those that the eye can see, that we can feel, and hear of, and conceive? Oh no. The greatest ills are those torments that never eye saw, that ear never heard of. It is to be in hell to know these things. They are beyond our conceit. 'The worm that dies not, fire unquenchable,' Mark ix. 43, the things above our apprehension are the most terrible things. It is not the gout or the stone. Men feel these things, and yet suffer them with some patience. These are not the greatest ills, but those of another world that are reserved for God's enemies; as the best things are those that are reserved for his friends.

Therefore let us make use of our understandings in laying things together, and make use of God's discovery of the state of Christianity, the excellencies of religion. Why doth God reveal these things in the word? That we should oft meditate of them, and study them, that we may be heavenly-minded. For there are none that come to heaven but they must have a taste of these beforehand. There are none ever [that] enjoy them in perfection. When the day of revelation shall come (the gospel now is the time of revelation, but the day of revelation is the time of judgment), then shall we be revealed what we are. But in the mean time there is a revelation by the Spirit in some beginnings of these things, or else we shall never come to have the perfection of them in heaven. If we know not what peace, and joy, and comfort, and the communion of the saints, and the change of nature is here in sanctification, we shall never know in heaven the fulfilling of it.

And those that have the first fruits here, if they be in a state of growth, that they desire to grow better continually, they shall, no question, come to the perfection; for God will not lose his beginnings. Where he gives earnest, he will make up the bargain.

Therefore let us all that know a little what these things are by the revelation of the Spirit, let us be glad of our portion. For God that hath begun, he will surely make an end.

The affection, and bent and frame of soul due to these things is admiration, and not only simple hearing. If these things in their beginnings here be set out by words of admiration, 'peace that passeth understanding,' and 'joy unspeakable and glorious,' what affection and frame of spirit is suitable to the hearing of those things that are kept for us in another world! If the light that we are brought into here is admirable, great (we are brought out of darkness into admirable wonderful light), if the light of grace be so wonderful to a man that comes out of the state of nature, as it is indeed (a man comes out of a damp into a wonderful clear light), what then is the light of glory! Therefore let us often think of it. Those that are born in a prison, they hear great talk of the light, and of the sun, of such a glorious creature; but being born in prison, they know not what it is in itself. So those that are in the prison of nature, they know not what the light of grace is. They hear talk of glorious things, and have conceits of them. And those that here know not the glory that shall be after, when they are revealed, that affection that is due to them is admiration and wonderment. 'So God loved the world, that he gave his only begotten Son,' John iii. 10; and 'Behold what love the Father hath showed to us, that we should be called the sons of God,' 1 John iii. 1. What love! He could not tell what, it is so admirable; and to know the love of God, that is above all knowledge! Who can comprehend the love of God, that gave his Son! Who can comprehend the excellency of Christ's gift! The joys of heaven by Christ, and the misery of hell, from which we are delivered and redeemed by Christ! These things come from the gospel, and the spring from whence they come is the large and infinite and incomprehensible love of God. And if it be so, what affection is answerable but admiration? Behold what love! If God have so loved flesh and blood, poor dust and ashes, so as to be heirs of heaven, and of such glory as eye sees not, nor cannot in this world; nor ear hears not; nor hath entered into the heart of man, till we come fully to possess them; let us labour to admire the love of God herein.

And labour to know more and more our inheritance, as we grow in years, as children do. They search into the great matters their parents leave them, and the nearer they come to enjoy them, the more skill they have to talk of them. So should we: the more we grow in Christianity and in knowledge, the more we should be inquisitive after those great things that our Father hath provided in another world. But to go on.

*How shall we know whether these things he prepared for us or no? whether we be capable of these things or no?* God hath prepared them, and he hath prepared them for those that love him; but how shall we know that God hath prepared them for us?

In a word, *whom God hath prepared great matters for, he prepares them for great matters.* We may know by God's preparing of us, whether he hath prepared for us. God prepared paradise before Adam was created: so God prepares paradise, he prepares heaven before we come there. And we may know that we shall come to possess that, if we be prepared for it. What preparation? If we be prepared by a spirit of sanctification, and have holy desires and longing after those excellent things; for certainly there is preparation on both sides. It is prepared for us, and us for it. It is kept for us, and we are kept for it. Whom God keeps heaven for, he keeps them for heaven in a course of piety and obedience. We may know it by God's preparing of us, by loosing us from the world, and sanctifying us to himself. Thus a man may know whether those great things be prepared for him or no.

But the especial thing to know whether they be provided for us or no is love. God hath prepared them for them that love him: not for his enemies. He hath prepared another place, and other things for them; those torments that 'eye hath not seen, nor ear heard, nor hath entered into the heart of man,' for those that are his enemies, that would not come under his government; but these things are prepared 'for those that love him.'

'For those that love him.' Especially that love is all in all, in the disposition of a holy man. All graces are one in the spring, which is love. They are several in the branches, but they are one in the root.

Thus you have heard the use we are to make of this, that there is a reservation of a glorious condition for the people of God so great that neither 'eye hath seen,' &c.

But who are the parties that God hath prepared these things for?

'For them that love him.'

This is the fourth part, the disposition of the parties for whom, 'for them that love him.'

*Quest. 1. Why not for those that God hath elected?* Why doth he not go to the root of all? The great things that God hath prepared for those that he hath chosen to salvation? No. *That is out of our reach.* He would not have us to go to heaven, but rather go to our own hearts. We must search for our election, not above ourselves, but within ourselves.

*Quest. 2. Why doth he not say, to them that believe in him, because faith is the radical grace from whence the rest spring?*

*Ans.* But faith is a hidden grace many times; and the apostle's scope is to point to such a disposition, that every one may know, that is more familiar. Sometimes faith is hidden in the root, and it is showed in the effect more than in itself, in love. A poor Christian that is in the state of grace, that saith, 'Oh, I cannot believe,' ask him if he love God. Oh yes; he loves the preaching of the word; he loves good people and good books, and the like. When he cannot discover his faith, he can his love. Therefore the Holy Ghost sets it out by the more familiar disposition, by love rather than faith.

*Quest. 3. Why doth he not say, For those that God loves?* God's love is the cause of our love.

*Ans. Because God's love is manifested more familiarly by our love to him*; for that is always supposed. Wheresoever there is love to God, and good things, there is God's love first. For our love to God is but a reflection of that love he bears to us. First, he shines on us, and then the beams of our love reflect upon him. Therefore he need not say, whom God loves (though that be the cause of all), but who love God; and know thereby that he loves them.

*Quest. 4. But why for them that love him more than for any other thing?*

*Ans. Because all can love.* Therefore he sets down this affection. There is no man living, not the poorest lazar[13] in the world, that hath a heart and affections, but he can love. He doth not say, that are prepared for this great Christian, and that learned Rabbi. No. But for all that love him, be they poor or rich, great or small, all those that love him. Therefore he sets down that to cut off all excuses. Yea, and all that love him, be they never so many, are sure to have these great things prepared for them. God hath 'prepared these things for those that love him.'

To come therefore to some observations. The first general thing is this, that,

*Obs. God doth qualify all those in this world, that he hath prepared heaven and happiness for in another world.*

The cause of it is his free love. But if you ask me what qualifications the persons must have? They are such as 'love him.' This is not the proper cause why, but the qualification of the persons for whom these things are. There must be an inward disposition and qualification, before we come to heaven. All those that hope for heaven without presumption must have this qualification, they must be such as 'love him.'

Why?

*Reasons.* The Scripture is plain, (1.) *No unclean thing shall enter into heaven.* No whoremonger, or drunkard, or filthy person. Be not deceived, saith the apostle, you think God is merciful, and Christ died, &c., but neither such, nor such as you are (and your consciences tell you so) shall ever enter into heaven, 1 Cor. vi. 9, *seq.* We must not think to come *è caeno in caelum*, out of the mire and dirt of sin into heaven. There is no such sudden getting into heaven; but there must be an alteration of our dispositions, wrought by the Spirit of God, fitting us for heaven.

(2.) Another is, that that I touched before, that *heaven and earth differ but in degrees, therefore what is there in perfection must be begun here.*

---

13 That is, 'diseased beggar like Lazarus.' —G.

(3.) Then again, thirdly, *it is impossible for a man, if he is not truly altered, to desire or wish heaven as it is holy*. He may wish for it under the notion of a kingdom, of pleasure, and the like; but as heaven contains a state of perfect holiness and freedom from sin, he cares not for it. A man that is out of relish with heavenly things, and can taste only his base sins, whereon his affections are set and exercised, cannot relish heaven itself. A common, base sinner, his desires are not there. There must be some proportion between the thing desired, and the desire. But here is none. He is not for that place, being an unholy wretch.

Therefore his own heart tells him, I had rather have this pleasure and honour that my heart stands to, than to have heaven, while he is in that frame of desire. Therefore there is no man that can desire heaven that is not disposed aright to heaven before. Beetles love dunghills better than ointments, and swine love mud better than a garden. They are in their element in these things. So take a swinish base creature, he loves to wallow in this world. Tell him of heaven: he hath no eyes to see it, no ears to hear it; except he may have that in heaven that his heart stands to (which he shall never have), he hath no desire of heaven. Therefore in these and the like respects, of necessity there must be a disposition wrought before we come there. These things are prepared for those that 'love God.'

*Use* 1. If this is so, *let us not feed ourselves with vain hopes*. There are none of us but we desire, at least we pretend that we desire, heaven; but most men conceive it only as a place free from trouble and annoyance; and they are goodly things they hear of, kingdoms, crowns, and the like. But except thou have a holy, gracious heart, and desirest heaven that thou mayest be free from sin, and to have communion with Christ and his saints, to have the image of God, the divine nature perfect in thee, thou art an hypocrite, thou carriest a presumptuous conceit of these things; thy hope will delude thee; it is a false hope. 'Every one that hath this hope purgeth himself,' 1 John iii. 3. Every one, he excludes none. Dost thou defile thyself, and live in sinful courses, and hast thou this hope? Thou hast a hope, but it is not this hope; for every one that hath this hope purgeth himself. No, no; however in time of peace, and pleasure, and contentment that God follows thee with in this world, thou hast a vain hope; yet in a little trouble, or sickness, &c., thy own conscience will tell thee another place is provided for thee, a place of torment, that nei-

ther 'eye hath seen nor ear heard, nor hath entered into
the heart of man to conceive' the misery of it. There is not
the greatest man living, when he is troubled, if he is a sinful man, whose greatness can content him. All his honour
and friends cannot pacify that poor conscience of his. But
death, 'the king of fears,' will affright him. He thinks, I
have some trouble in this world, but there is worse that
remains; things that he is not able to conceive of. Let us
not therefore delude ourselves. There is nothing will stand
out but the new creature, that we find a change wrought
by the Spirit of God. Then we may without presumption
hope for the good things which neither 'eye hath seen,' &c.

*Use* 2. Again, we see in the second place God's mercy to us; the qualification is within us, that we need not,
go far to know what our evidence is. Satan abuseth many
poor Christians. Oh I am not elected, I am not the child of
God! Whither goest thou, man? Dost thou break into heav-
en? When thou carriest a soul in thy breast, and in that
soul the affection of love; how is that sot? Whither is thy
love carried, and thy delight, and joy, those affections that
spring from love? Thy evidence is in thine own heart. Our
title is by faith in Christ. His righteousness gives us title to
heaven. But how knowest thou that thou pretendest a just
title? Thou hast the evidence in thy heart. What is the bent
of thy soul? Whither is the point of it set? Which way goeth
that? Dost thou love God, and divine things, and delight
in them? Then thou mayest assure thyself that those things
belong to thee, as verily as the Scriptures are the word of
God, and God a God of truth. When thou findest the love
of God in thy heart, that thy heart is taught by his Spirit to
love him, then surely thou mayest say, Oh blessed be God
that hath kindled this holy fire in my heart. Now I know
that 'neither eye hath seen, nor ear heard, nor hath entered
into the heart of man, those excellent things that are laid
up for me.'

# THE THIRD SERMON

*Eye hath not seen, &c.*
1 Cor. ii. 9.

Saint Paul, as we heard before, gives a reason in these words, why the 'princes of this world' (not only the great men, that ofttimes are not the greatest clerks,[14] but the learned men of the world, princes for knowledge), why they were ignorant of the mysteries of the gospel.

Now the fourth is the disposition of those for whom he doth all this; the quality he infuseth into them, they are such as 'love him.'

1. *He hath prepared them before all eternity.* He prepared happiness for us before we were; nay, before the world was. As he prepared for Adam a paradise before he was; he created him, and then brought him into paradise: so he prepared for us a kingdom with himself in heaven, a blessed estate before we were; i.e., in election, before the heavens were. And then in creation he prepared the blessed place of the happy souls of happy persons hereafter, where he himself is. He prepared it for himself, and for all those that he means to set his love upon from the beginning to the end.

2. And then, *secondly*, he prepared them *more effectually in time*. He prepared these things when Christ came in the flesh, and wrought all things for us, in whom we have all. Of these things thus prepared he saith, 'Eye hath not seen, nor ear heard them,' &c. In what sense it is meant we heard before. Now take the whole of the matter; the meaning is, *the matters of grace, the kingdom of grace, and the kingdom of glory, they are but one.* For (to add this by the way) the kingdom of heaven in the gospel includes three things.

*First*, The doctrine of the gospel, the publishing of it.

And then, *secondly*, Grace by that doctrine.

And *thirdly*, Glory upon grace, the consummation of

---

14  That is, 'scholars.' —G.

all.

So the mysteries of salvation is, first, the doctrine itself. That is the first degree of the kingdom. The doctrine itself is a mystery to all those that never heard of it; for what creature could ever conceive how to reconcile justice and mercy, by devising such a way as for God to become man, to reconcile God and man together? That Immanuel, he that is 'God with us,' should make God and us one in love, this could be no more thought of, than Adam could think of himself to be made a man when he was dust of the earth. Could man when he was worse than dust, in a lost, damned estate, think of redemption? It is impossible for a man that cannot tell the form and the quintessence, that cannot enter into the depth of the flowers, or the grass that he tramples on with his feet, that he should have the wit[15] to enter into the deep things of God, that have been concealed even from the angels themselves till God discover them. I add this to illustrate what I said before. Therefore the doctrine itself, till God discover it out of his own breast, was concealed to the angels themselves; and since the discovery, they are students in it, and look and pry into it, 1 Peter i. 12. But where the doctrine is no mystery, but is discovered, there the application and spiritual understanding, to those that have not the light of the Spirit, is such a thing as 'eye hath not seen nor ear heard.' And therefore we must have a new light, a new eye, a new ear, and a new heart, before we can apprehend the gospel, though we understand it for the literal truth. As for the things of glory, we have no conceit of them fully, but by a glimpse and weak apprehension; as a child conceives of the things of a man, by some poor weak resemblances. As St Paul saith, 'When I was a child I spoke as a child, I thought as a child,' 1 Cor. xiii. 11. So when we are now children, in comparison of that perfect estate we shall attain in heaven, we think and speak as children, of these holy and heavenly things that shall be accomplished in another world.

And observe this too, that when we would understand anything of heaven, and see anything, say, 'This is not that happiness I look for,' 'I can see this, but that is not to be seen.' And when we hear of anything that is excellent, 'I can hear this, it is not my happiness.' And when we comprehend anything, 'I can comprehend this;' therefore it is not the happiness I look for, but those things that

---

15  That is, 'wisdom.'—G.

are above my comprehension, that are unutterable and inexpressible.

Moreover, *let us be stirred up to think it a base thing for a Christian to lose the comfort and assurance he hath of these things* 'that eye hath not seen nor ear heard,' *for any earthly thing whatsoever*. We account it a poor thing of Esau to sell his birthright for a mess of pottage, Heb. xii. 16. And we all smart for Adam's ill bargain that he made, to sell paradise for an apple. And it was a cursed sale that Judas made, that sold Christ himself for thirty pieces of silver. Surely it is that that every carnal man doth; and howsoever we cannot lose heaven, yet it should be our endeavour to enjoy heaven upon earth, to enjoy the assurance of this condition. When we do anything to weaken our assurance, and to weaken our comfort, what do we but with Adam lose heaven for an apple, and with Esau part with our birthright, as much as the assurance and comfort of it is, for a mess of pottage? Therefore let us account it a base thing to be over-much in love with any earthly thing, whereby we may weaken (though we could not lose) the comfort and assurance of this happy condition, which is so transcendent. All wicked men, and indeed all men whether good or bad, as far as they fall into sin, are fools; the Scripture terms them so. There is none wise indeed but the true Christian, and that Christian that preserves the sense, and feeling, and assurance of his happy condition.

'For those that love him.'

The disposition of the parties is, they are such as 'love God.' He saith not, such as are elected, because that is a thing out of our reach to know; but by going upward, by going backward, to go from our grace to our calling, and from thence to election; nor such as believe, because that is less discernible than love; nor the love of God to us, for that is supposed when we love him. Our hearts being cold, they cannot be warm in love to him, but his love must warm them first. Love is such an affection as commands all other things, therefore he names that above all. And love is such a thing as every one may try himself by. If he had named either giving or doing of this or that, men might have said, I cannot do it, or I cannot part with it, but when he names love, there is none but they may love. The point considered was, that *there must be a qualification of those that heaven is provided for*.

They must be such as love God, such as are altered, and changed, and sanctified to love him; because no unclean thing shall enter in thither; because we cannot so much as desire heaven without a change. We cannot have communion there with Christ and those blessed souls without likeness to them, which must be by a spirit of love; our natures must be altered. Therefore it is a vain presumption for any man to think of heaven unless he find his disposition altered. For we may read our eternal condition in heaven by our disposition upon earth. The apostle Peter saith, 1 Pet. i. 3, 'Blessed be God, the Father of our Lord Jesus Christ, that hath begotten us to a lively hope of an inheritance immortal and undefiled, reserved in heaven.' So that the inheritance in heaven, we are begotten to it; we must be new born; we must have a new birth before we can inherit it; 'He hath begotten us to an inheritance immortal,' &c. He that is not a child may not think of an inheritance. Put case there be never so many glorious things in heaven that 'eye hath never seen nor ear ever heard,' &c., if our names be not in Christ's will, that we are not his, and prove ourselves to be his, by the alteration of our dispositions, what are all those good things to us, when our names are not contained there!

It is called a hope of life, 'a lively hope,' 1 Pet. i. 3; because he that hath this 'hope purgeth himself.' It makes him vigorous and active in good. If his hope of life make him not lively, he hath no hope of life at all. Therefore those that will look for heaven (that Satan abuse them not by false confidence), let them look whether God have altered their hearts; that the work of grace be wrought in some measure. For God hath not ordained these great things for his enemies; for blasphemers, that take God's name in vain; that run on in courses contrary to his will and word; that live in sins against the light of nature; do you think he hath provided these great matters for them? He hath another place for them. Therefore let us not be abused by our own false hearts to think of such a happy condition. Unless we find ourselves changed, unless we be new born, we shall never enter into heaven.

'Lord, Lord,' say they. Christ brings them in pleading so, 'Lord, Lord;' not that they shall say so then, that is not the meaning; but now they cherish such a confidence. Oh we can speak well, and we can pray well, 'Lord, Lord.' Oh thou vain, confident person, thy confession and profession, 'Lord, Lord,' shall do thee no good. I will not so much as own thee; 'Away hence, thou worker of iniquity,' Matt. xxv. 41. Thy heart tells thee thou livest in sins against

conscience. Away, avaunt, I will [have] none of thee. God
in mercy to us will have the trial of the truth of our evidence in us. The ground of all our salvation is his grace, his
free favour, and mercy in his own heart; but we cannot go
thither; he would have us to search within ourselves, and
there we shall find 'love.'

'God hath prepared for those that love him.'

*Obs.* In particular, therefore, *those that God hath provid-*
*ed so excellent things for, they are such as love him.* They are
such, first of all, that are beloved of him; and show that
they are beloved of him by their love to him. Therefore,
when the papists meet with such phrases, they think of
merit. He hath provided heaven for them that love him,
and show their love in good works. But we must know
that this is not brought in as a cause why, but as a qualification of the persons who; who shall inherit heaven, and
who shall have these great things. It is idle for them to
think that these things are prepared for those whom God
foresees would do such and such good works. It is as if
we should think he hath provided these happy things for
those that are his enemies. For how could he look for love
from us in a state of corruption, when the best thing in us
was enmity to him? Is it not a vain thing to look for light
from darkness? To look for love from enmity and hatred?
Therefore how could God foresee anything in us, when he
could see nothing but enmity and darkness in our dispositions by nature?

And then (as we shall see afterward) this love in us
it must be with all our heart, and soul, and might. It is
required and commanded; and when we do all this, we do
but what we are bound to do. But they abuse such places
upon so shallow ground, that indeed it deserves not so
much as to be mentioned.

To come then to the point itself, *the disposition of those*
*that shall come to heaven then is, they must be such as love God.*
Now he names this because these two go always together. There goes somewhat of ours together with somewhat
of God's, to witness to us what God doth. There goes our
choice of God, with his choosing of us; our knowing of
God, with his knowledge of us; our love to him, with his
love to us. Therefore, because these are so connected and
knit together, he takes the one for the other; and to make
it familiar to us, he takes that which is most familiar to us,
our love to him.

Now he names this above all other affections, because

love is the commanding affection of the soul. It is that affection that rules all other affections. Hatred, and anger, and joy, and delight, and desire, they all spring from love; and because all duties spring from love both to God and man, therefore both tables are included in love. And when the apostle would set down the qualifications of those that shall enjoy these things, he saith they are for those 'that love him.' Because it stirs up to all duty, and adds a sweet qualification to every duty, and makes it acceptable and to relish with God. It stirs up to do, and qualifies the actions that come from love to be accepted.

All duties to man spring from love to man, and love to man from love to God. It is the affection that stirs up the duty, and stirs up the affection fit for the duty; it stirs up to do the thing, and to do all in love. Whatsoever we do to God or man, it must be in love. All that God doth to us it is in love. He chooseth us in love, and doth everything in love; and all that we do to God it must be in love. Therefore he names no other affection but this, because it is the ground, the first-born affection of the soul. Therefore Christ saith it is the great commandment to love God, John xv. 12. It is the great commanding commandment, that commands all other duties whatsoever; it is the first wheel that turns the whole soul about.

Again, it is such an affection as cannot be dissembled. A man may paint fire, but he cannot paint heat. A man may dissemble actions in religion, but he cannot affections. Love is the very best affection of truth. A man may counterfeit actions; but there is none that can love but the child of God. 'God hath prepared these things for those that *love him.'*

Then again, without this, all that we do is nothing, and we are nothing. We are nothing but an empty cymbal. Whatsoever we do is nothing; all is empty without love. 'My son, give me thy heart,' Prov. xxiii. 26; that is, if thou wilt give me anything, give me thy affections, or else they are still-born actions, that have no life in them. If we do anything to God, and do it not in love, he regards it not. That is the reason why he mentions love instead of all. It is so sweet an affection, and so easy; what is more easy than to love? It is comfortable to us to consider that God hath made this a qualification of those that he brings to heaven; they are such as 'love him.'

*Quest.* But why doth he set down any qualification at all, and not say, *for Christians?*

*Ans.* Because *profession must have expression.* When God sets down a professor of religion, he sets him down by some character that shall discover him to be as he is termed. How dost thou know thou art good? Dost thou love God, or call upon God? as it is in other places, 'To all those that call upon his name,' 1 Cor. i. 2, to let us know that religion and holiness is a matter of power. Wouldst thou know what thou art in religion? Dost thou love God, or call upon God?

It is not to be tolerated, to be Christians, to profess as Demas, 2 Tim. iv. 10. Oh no! but they must be such as from the heart-root are good, 'such as love God.'

Therefore, dark disputes of election and predestination, at the first especially, let them go. How standest thou affected to God and to good things? Look to thy heart whether God have taught it to love or no, and to relish heavenly things. If he hath, thy state is good. And then thou mayest ascend to those great matters of predestination and election. But begin not with those, but go first to thine own heart, and then to those deep mysteries afterward. If a man love God, he may look back to election, and forward to glorification, to the things that 'eye hath not seen nor ear heard,' &c. But see first what God hath wrought in thy heart, what affection to heavenly things; and thence from thy affections to go backward to election, and forward to glorification, there is no danger in it.

To come therefore to express more particularly this affection of love, which is the disposition that God requires and works in all those that he intends heaven to. Let us search into the nature of this love to God. What it is to love we need not be taught, for all men know it well enough. It is better known, indeed, by the affection than by discourse. What it is to love is known by those that love better than by any books or treatises whatsoever, for it is the affection that is in all men. Natural love, it is in those that have no grace at all, and civil love in those that are evil men. They know what it is to love by reason of that wild fire, that carnal love that is in them, that transports them. A man may see the nature of it in those as well as in any; for set aside the extravagant nature of it in such kind of persons, we may see the nature of it. Therefore I will not meddle with that point; it is *needless.* I come therefore to this love of God, *to* show how this stream of affection should be carried in the right channel to God, the right object of it, who only can make us happy by loving of him. Other things, by loving of them, they make us worse, if they be worse than ourselves; for such as we love, such we are. Indeed, our understandings make us not good or ill, but our love doth. By loving God and heavenly things we become good. Our affections show what we are in religion.[16]

There are four things in this sweet affection in true natural love.

1. *There is an estimation and valuing of some good thing, especially when the love is to a better, when it is not between equals.* Now there is a great distance between God and us. There is a high esteem in common love; love will not stoop to nothing. There cannot be love maintained but upon sight of a supposed excellency; love will not stoop but where it sees somewhat worth the valuing. Therefore there is a high esteem of somewhat as the spring of it. And that is the reason that we say a man cannot be wise and love in earthly things, because love will make a man too much to value those things that he that apprehends better would not.

2. In the *second* place, *there is a desire to be joined to it, that we call the desire of union.*

3. In the *third* place, upon union and joining to it, *there is a resting, a complacency and contentment in the thing to which we are united,* for what is happiness itself but fully to enjoy what we love? When we love upon judgment and a right esteem, to enjoy, that is happiness and contentment indeed.

4. In the *fourth* place, where this true affection is, *there is a desire of contentment to the party loved, to please him, to approve ourselves to him, to displease him in nothing.* Every one knows that these things are in that affection by nature.

Look to carnal self-love, a man may know what it is to love; the affection is all one in both. Take a man when he makes himself his idol, as till a man love God he loves himself above all, he is the idol and the idolater; he hath a high esteem of himself, and those that do not highly esteem him he swells against them. Again, self-love makes a man desire to enjoy himself, and to enjoy his content, to procure all things that may serve for his contentment.

Now, when the Spirit of God hath purged our hearts of this carnal idolatry of self-love, and self-seeking, and sufficiency, and contentment in himself, then a man puts God instead of himself; grace, and the Spirit doth so; and instead of highly esteeming of himself, he esteems highly

---

16  Cf. President Edwards' treatise on 'The *Religious Affections.*' —G.

of God, and of Christ, and religion. Then, instead of placing a sufficiency in himself and the things of this life, and resting in them, there is a placing of sufficiency in God all-sufficient. And instead of seeking his own will and content in all things, *mens mihi pro regno,* my mind is to me a kingdom, then a man seeks to give contentment to God in all things, and 'to be a fool, that he may be wise,' 1 Cor. iii. 18, and to have no will and no delight in anything that cannot stand with the pleasure of and obedience to God.

Thus a man, by knowing what his own natural corruption is, he may know what his affection is to better things.

First of all, *there must be an estimation, an esteem of God and Christ*; for to avoid misconceit, we take both these to be one: God our Father in Christ, and Christ. Whatsoever Christ did for us in love, he did it from the love of the Father who gave him. And when we speak of the love of God, we speak of the love of Christ to us. Therefore there must be a high esteeming, and valuing, and prizing of God above all things in the world, and of his love.

(1.) Now, this must needs be so; for where grace is, it gives a sanctified judgment; a sanctified judgment values and esteems things as they are. Now the judgment, apprehending God and his love to be the best thing to make us happy, prizeth it above all: 'Whom have I in heaven but thee? and what have I in earth in comparison of thee?' Ps. lxxiii. 25. He prizeth God and his love above all things in the world.

Now, if we would know if we have this judgment, we may know it by our choice. This valuing it is known by choice: for what a man esteems and values highly he makes choice of above all things in the world. What men make choice of is seen by their courses. We see it in holy Moses, Heb. xi. 26, *seq.* He had a high esteem of the estate of God's people, that afflicted people. As afflicted as they were, yet he saw they were God's people, in covenant with him, and more regarded of him than all the people in the world besides; and upon his estimation he made a choice: 'he chose rather to suffer afflictions with the people of God, than to enjoy the pleasures of sin for a season.' His choice followed his esteem. So if we value and esteem God and religion, and love God above all things, we will make choice of the Lord. As St Peter saith, John vi. 68, *seq.,* when Christ asked them, 'Will ye also forsake me?' saith he, 'Lord, whither shall we go?' We have made choice of thee;

'whither shall we go? thou hast the words of eternal life.' Let us do that in truth that he for a time failed to do, when he said, 'Though all forsake thee, yet will not I,' Matt. xxvi. 33. If we make this choice of Christ from the truth of our hearts, this shows our esteem.

What is thy choice? Is it religious ways and religious company? Is it the fear of God above all things? 'One thing have I desired, that I may dwell in the house of God for ever, and visit his temple,' Ps. xxvii. 4. Hast thou with Mary made choice of the better part? Dost thou value thyself as a member of Christ, and an heir of heaven, as a Christian above all conditions in this world (for what a man esteems he values himself by)? Then thou art a true lover, thou hast this love planted in thy heart, because thou hast a true esteem. You see Paul accounted 'all dung and dross in comparison of the excellent knowledge of Christ,' Philip. iii. 8. Oh that we could come to that excellent affection of St Paul, to undervalue all things to Christ, and the good things by Christ and religion! Certainly it is universally true, where Christ is loved, and God in Christ, the price of all things else fall in the soul. For when we welcome Christ, then farewell all that cannot stand with Christ.

(2.) Again, our esteem is known *by our willing parting with anything for that that we esteem*; as a wise merchant doth sell all for the pearl, Matt. xiii. 46. We may know therefore that we esteem God and his truth; for they go together, God and his truth and religion. We must take God with all that he is clothed with, wherein he shows himself unto us. If we sell all for the truth of God, and part with all, and deny all for the love and obedience of it, it is a sign we have an esteem answerable to his worth, and that we love him.

Those therefore that will part with nothing for God, nor for religion and the truth, when they are called to it, do they talk of love to God? They have no esteem, they value not God. If they did esteem him, they would sell all for the pearl. Therefore those that halt in religion, that care not which way religion and the truth goes, so they may have honour and pleasures in this world, where is their esteem of the gospel, and of the truth of Christ and of God? They have no love, because they have no estimation.

(3.) Again, what we esteem highly of *we speak largely of*. A man is always eloquent in that he esteems. It will put him, to the extent of his abilities, to be as eloquent as possible he can be. You never knew a man want words for that he prized, to set it out. Therefore when we want words to praise God, and to set out the value of the best things, it is an argument we have poor esteem of them. All go together, God and the things of God. What! do we talk of loving God, and despise Christians and religion? They are never severed. If a man esteem the best things, he will be often speaking of them. If a man set his affections upon a thing, it will suggest words at will. Therefore those that are clean out of their theme, when they speak of good things, are to seek, Alas! where is the affection of love? where is esteem? Esteem it makes a readiness to speak.

(4.) Esteem likewise *carries our thoughts*. Wouldst thou know what thou esteemest highly? What dost thou think of most and highest? Thou mayest know it by that. We see the first branch, how we may know we love God, if we have a high esteem and valuing of God, by these signs.

*Secondly*, Where there is true love and affection, *there is a desire of union*; of knitting and coupling with the thing loved. Of necessity it must be so; for love is such a kind of affection, it draws the soul all it can to the thing loved. It hath a magnetical force, the force of a loadstone. Every one knows what this means.

This affection of love makes us one with that we love. If a man love the world, he is a worldling, a man of the world, because affection breeds union. Though a man be never so base in choosing, whatsoever a man loves he desires union with it; and being so, he hath his name from that he loves. He that loves the world is a worldling, an earthworm. Now, if there is the love of God, as in covenant, as a Father in Christ, for so we must conceive of God, there will be a desire of fellowship and communion with him by all means, in the word and sacrament, &c. If a man desire strangeness, that he cares not how seldom he receive the sacrament or come into God's presence, is here love? How can love and strangeness stand together? Thou art a strange person from God, and the things of God; thou hast no joy in his presence. Where thou mayest enjoy his presence here in holy things in this world, if thou delight not in his presence and in union with him, how canst thou say thou lovest him?

Can a man say he loves him whose company he cares not for? Thou carest not for God's company. Thou mayest meet him in the word and sacraments, and in good company: 'Where two or three are gathered together, I will be in the midst,' Matt. xviii. 20. Dost thou pretend thou lovest

God if thou carest not for these? Thou hast no fellowship in this business; all that relish not heavenly things, they do not love.

Now, to try whether we have this branch of love, that is, a desire of union. Where therefore there is a desire of union with the party loved, of uniting to that person (for we speak of persons), there will be a desire of communion.

(1.) *A desire of union will breed a desire of communion;* that is, there will be a course taken to open our minds. If we have a desire of communion with God, we will open our souls often to him in prayer, and we will desire that he will open himself in speaking to our hearts by his Spirit. And we will desire that he will open his mind to us in his word. We will be careful to hear his word, and so maintain that sweet and heavenly commerce between him and our souls by this intercourse of hearing him and speaking to him: 'Where two or three are gathered together, I will be in the midst.' Therefore those that make no conscience either of hearing the word, or of prayer public and private, and of using the glorious liberty that we have in Christ, of free access to the throne of grace, that do not use this prerogative and privilege to cherish that union and communion they may have with God, they love not God and Christ. Strangeness is opposite to love, and it dissolves and disunites affections. Therefore when we are strange to God, that we can go from one end of the week to the other, and from the beginning of the day to the end of it, and not be acquainted with God, and not open our souls to him, it is a sign we have no love; because there is no desire of union and communion with him.

(2.) Again, where we love *we consult and advise, and rest in that advice, as coming from a loving person,* especially if he be as wise as loving. So in all our consultations, we will go to God and take his counsel; and when we have it, we will account it the counsel of one that is wise and loving.

Those therefore that trust to their own wits, to policy and such like, what do they speak of love when they make not use of that covenant that is between God and them? They consult not with him; they make not his word the 'man of their counsel,' Ps. cxix. 24; They go not to him by prayer for advice; they commit not their 'ways' to him, as the psalmist speaketh, Ps. xxxvii. 5.

(3.) And this distinguished a good Christian from another man: *a good Christian he is such a one as acquaints himself with his God, and will not lose that intercourse he hath with God for all the world.* As Daniel, he would not but pray; they could not get him from it with the hazard of his life, Dan. vi. 11.

(4.) Again, where this desire of union and joining is, *there is a desire even of death itself, that there may be a fuller union, and a desire of the consummation of all things.* Therefore so far as we are afraid of death, and tremble at it, so far we want love. When the contract is once made between Christ and the soul of a Christian, for him to fear the making up of the marriage, when we are now absent from the Lord, to fear the sweet eternal communion we shall have in heaven, where we shall have all things in greater excellency and abundance, it is from want of faith and love. Therefore we should be ashamed of ourselves when we find such thoughts rising in our hearts, as they will naturally, to be basely and distrustfully afraid of death. St Paul saith, 'I desire to be dissolved, and to be with Christ;' that is good, nay, it is much better for me, Philip. i. 23. Nay, it is best of all to be with Christ. Therefore, you see, it stirred up his desire: 'I desire to be dissolved, and to be with Christ.' 'Come, Lord Jesus; come quickly,' saith the church, Rev. xxii. 20. And the Spirit in the spouse stirs up this desire likewise: 'Come; the Spirit and the spouse say, Come,' Rev. xxii. 17. And we should rejoice to think there are happier times to come, wherein there will be an eternal meeting together that nothing shall dissolve, as the apostle saith, 1 Thes. iv. 17, 'when we shall he for ever with the Lord.' Oh those times cheer up the heart of a Christian beforehand!

Now where these things possess not the soul, how can we say that we love God? In Cant. i. 1 the church begins, 'Let him kiss me with the kisses of his mouth.' She desires a familiar communion with Christ in his word and ordinances, 'Let him kiss me,' &c. Let him speak by his Spirit to my heart. In this world Christ kisseth his church with the kisses of his mouth. But in the latter end of the Canticles, 'Make haste, my beloved,' viii. 14, she desires his second coming, thinks it not enough to have the kisses of his mouth; 'Make haste, my beloved, and be as the young roes upon the mountains of spices;' that is, come hastily from heaven, the mountain of spices, and let us meet together, my beloved. These things be somewhat strange to our carnal dispositions, but if we hope ever to attain to the comfort of what I say, we must labour that our hearts may be brought to this excellent condition, to desire the presence of Christ. That is the second property of love.

The *third* is *to rest pleased and contented in the thing when we are joined with it*; so far as we are joined with it to place our contentment in it. And it is in the nature of that affection to place contentment in the thing we desire to have, when we have it once.

Now we may know this our contentment whether we rest in God or no by the inward quiet and peace of the soul in all conditions, when whatsoever our condition be in this world, yet we know we have the light of God's countenance, and can rest and be content in it more than worldly men in their corn and wine and oil, as David saith, Ps. iv. 7, 'I rejoice more in the light of thy countenance, than when they have their corn and wine and oil;' when we can joy and solace ourselves with the assurance of God's favour and love in Jesus Christ. 'Being justified by faith, we have peace with God,' and rejoice in God, as it is Rom. v. 1; we rejoice in God as ours.

Therefore those that go to outward contentments, that run out to them as if there were not enough in God and divine things to content their souls, but they must be beholding to the devil and to the flesh, this is not to rest in God. He is over-covetous whom God cannot content. If we be in covenant with him, he is able to fill our soul, and all the corners of it; he is able to satisfy all the delights and desires of it; he is a gracious Father in Christ. Whither should we go from him for contentment? Why should we go out of religion to content ourselves in vain recreations and pleasures of sin for a season, when we have abundance in God?

And where there is contentment, there will be trusting in him and relying upon him. A man will not rely upon riches, or friends, or anything; for where we place our contentment, we place our trust. So far as we love God, so far we repose affiance[17] and trust in him; he will be our rock and castle and strength. Wouldst thou know whether thou restest in him or no? In the time of danger, whither doth thy soul run? To thy purse if thou be a rich man? Or to thy friends if thou be a worldly-minded man? Every man hath his castle to fly to. But 'the name of the Lord is a strong tower,' Ps. lxi. 3. He that is a child of God flieth thither for refuge, and there he covereth himself, and is safe. He enters into those chambers of divine providence and goodness, and there he rests in all troubles.

---

17  That is, 'Trust, confidence.'

Therefore ask thy affections whither thou wouldst run if there come a confusion of all things. When men are apt to say, Oh what will become of us! and they think of this and that, a good Christian hath God to rest in. He hath God reconciled in Christ, and in his love he plants himself in life and death. He makes God his habitation and his castle, as it is Ps. xviii. 2, 'I love the Lord dearly, my rock and my fortress.' And Moses in Ps. xc. 1, *seq.* (for his psalm it is), 'Thou hast been our habitation from everlasting to everlasting.' We dwell in thee. Though in the world we are tossed up and down, and live and die, yet we alway dwell with thee. So a Christian hath his contentment and his habitation in God; he is his house he dwells in, his rock, his resting-place, his centre in which he rests. 'Come unto me, and ye shall find rest to your souls,' Matt. xi. 28. When a man is beat out of all contentments, he may know by this whether he love God or no. As David when he was beat out of all, and they were ready to stone him; but 'he trusted in the Lord his God,' Ps. xxvi. 1, *et alibi.* So in losses and crosses hast thou contentment in God, thou wilt fetch what thou losest out of the love of God, and what thou art crossed in thou wilt fetch out of God's love. Thou wilt say, This and that is taken from me, but God is mine; I can fetch more good by faith from him than I can lose in the world. A soul that is acquainted with God, when he loseth anything in the world, he can fetch it out of the fountain and spring. He is taught to love God; he is skilful this way to pitch his hope and affiance in God, where he hath enough for all crosses. Let us labour to bring our souls more and more to this, and then we shall know what it is to love God by this placing of our contentment in him. 'Take all from me,' saith holy Austin, 'so thou leave me thyself'. So a Christian can say, Take all from me, so I have God.

Indeed, where shall a man have comfort in many passages of his life, if he find it not in religion? What will become of a man in this uncertain world, if he have not somewhat where he may place his content? Oh, he will find before he die that he is a wretched man. He knows not where to find rest and contentment before he dies; he will be beat out of all his holds here either by sickness or one thing or other.

The *fourth* and last is, *where the true affection of love to God is, it stirs up the soul to give all contentment to God, to do all things that may please him.* This is the nature of love. It stirs up to please the party loved. Isaac's sons saw that

their father loved venison, therefore they provided venison for him, Gen. xxv. 28. Those that know what God loves
will provide what they can that that God may delight
in. He loves a humble and a believing heart. 'Thou hast
wounded me with one of thine eyes,' Cant. iv. 9—the eye
of faith, when the soul can trust in the word, and humbly
go out of itself. His delight is in a broken yielding heart,
that hardens not itself against his instructions, but yields.
A broken heart that lies low, and hears all that God saith,
Oh 'it is a sacrifice that God is much delighted in,' Ps. li.
17, *et alibi*. A humble spirit is such a spirit as God dwells in.
'He that dwells in the highest heavens dwells in a humble
spirit,' Isa. lvii. 15. Doth God delight in a meek, broken,
humble spirit? Oh then it will be the desire of a Christian
to have such a spirit as God may delight in. A meek soul is
much esteemed; 'the hidden man of the heart,' 1 Pet. iii. 4,
is much prized. Search in God's word what he delights in,
and let us labour to bring ourselves to such a condition as
God may delight in us, and we in him. And then it is a sign
we love him, when we labour to procure all things that
may give him content. You know that love where it is, it
stirs up the affections of the party to remove all things that
are distasteful to the party it loves. Therefore it is a neat
[18]affection; for it will make those neat that otherwise are
not so, because it will not offend; much more this divine
heavenly affection, when it is set on a right object, upon
God, it is a neat, cleanly affection. It will purge the soul; it
will work upon the soul a desire to be clean as much as can
be, because God is a pure, holy God, and it will 'have no
fellowship with the works of darkness,' Eph. v. 11. Therefore as much as human frailty will permit, it will study
purity, to keep itself 'unspotted of the world,' James i. 27.
It will not willingly cherish any sin that may offend the
Spirit. Those therefore that are careless of their ways and
carriage and affections, that make nothing of polluting,
and defiling their affections and their ways, there is not the
love of God in their hearts. It stirs up shame to be offensive
in the eyes of such a one, especially if they be great. There
is both love and respect met together. Where it is a rever-
ential love with respect, there is a shame to be in a base,
filthy, displeasing condition. God hates pride and idolatry, &c. Therefore a man that loves God will hate idols
and all false doctrine and worship that tends this way. His
heart will rise against them, because he knows God hates

---

18   That is, = nice, clean, opposed to filthy.

it, and all that take that course. He observes what is most offensive to God, and he will avoid it and seek what is pleasing to him.

God and Christ are wondrously pleased with faith. 'Thou hast wounded me with one of thine eyes.' Faith, and love from faith, wounds the breast of Christ: therefore let us labour for faith. 'O woman, great is thy faith,' Matt. xv. 28. It is such a grace as binds and overcomes God, it honours him so much. Let us therefore labour for faith, and in believing, for all graces. They are things that God loves. Therefore let us labour to be furnished with all things that he loves. Especially those graces that have some excellency set upon them in the Scripture we should most esteem. Isaac, when he was to marry Rebecca, he sends her jewels beforehand, that having them, she might be more lovely in his eye, Matt. xv. 28. So Christ, the husband of his church, that he might take more delight and content in his church, he sends her jewels beforehand; that is, he enricheth his church with the spirit of faith, meekness, humility, and love, and all graces, that he may delight and take content in his spouse. Those that have not somewhat that God may delight in them, they have not the spirit of love. Those, therefore, that rebel instead of giving God content; that resist the Spirit, and the motions of it, in the ministry, and in reprehensions, and the like: those that live in sins directly against God's command, that are common swearers, and filthy persons, neglecters of holy things, profane, godless persons, do they talk of the love of God and of heaven? You may see the filthiness of their hearts by the filthiness that issues from them. God keeps not such excellencies for such persons. The love of God, and living in sins against conscience, will not stand together. A demonstration of love is *exhibitio operis*, the exhibition of somewhat to please God. Show me in thy course what thou doest to please God. If thou live in courses that are condemned, never talk of love. It is a pitiful thing to see in the bosom of the church, under the glorious revelation of divine truth, that men should live apparently[19] and impudently in sins against conscience, that glory in their shame. It is a strange thing that they should glory in their profaneness and swaggering; that they should glory in a kind of atheistical carriage. As they have been bred, so they will be still. Many are marred in that; they are either poisoned in their first breeding, or neglected in it.

---

19   That is, 'Openly.' —G.

To see under the glorious gospel of Christ, that those
that think they have souls eternal, that they should live
in impudent base courses, void of religion and humanity,
only to satisfy their own lusts, instead of satisfying and
obeying God; men that live in the bosom of the church as
beasts, and yet hope to be saved as well as the best; Oh, but
the hope of the hypocrite, the hope of such persons, will
deceive them.

Oh let us labour therefore to have this affection of love
planted in our hearts; that God by his Spirit would teach
us to love him, and to love one another. This affection of
love must he taught by God. It is not a matter of the brain
to teach that, but a matter of the heart. God only is the
great schoolmaster and teacher of the heart. He must not
only command us to love, but teach our affections by his
Holy Spirit, to enable our affections to love him.

Where love is in this regard likewise to give content,
there will be love of all those whom the party we approve
ourselves to loves. Is there any of Jonathan's posterity,
saith David, that I may do good to them for his sake? 2
Sam. ix. 1. The soul that loves God and Christ saith, Is
there any good people, any that carry the image of God
and Christ? It will be sure to love them. It will do good to
Jonathan's posterity. Those that hate them that carry the
image of God and Christ, that their stomach riseth against
good men, how do they 'love him that begets, when they
love not him that is begotten?' 1 John v. 1. There cannot
be the love of God in such a man. Undoubtedly if we love
God, we shall love his children, and anything that hath
God's stamp upon it. We shall love his truth and his cause
and religion, and whatsoever is divine and toucheth upon
God. We shall love it, because it is his. It is such an affection as sets the soul on work to think, Wherein may I
give content to such a person? It is full of devices and inventions to please. Therefore it thinks, Can I give consent
in loving such and such? As Christ saith, he that respects
these little ones, it is to me, it is accountable on my part, I
will see it answered, Matt. xviii. 5. If the love of Christ be in
us, we will regard this, because we will think: Christ will
regard me for the good I do for his sake, and in his name,
to this and that party. Thus we see how we may try this
sweet affection, and not deceive our own souls.

And therefore, where there is a desire of giving content, there will be a zeal against all things; to remove all
things in our places and callings that may offend. It will

carry us through all difficulties. To please him, it will make us willing to suffer. I will please him, by suffering some indignity for his cause. I will do it, that I may engage his affection to me. Therefore the disciples gloried in this, when they were thought worthy to suffer for Christ's sake, Acts v. 41. Where there is a desire to please God, it is so far from being ashamed or afraid to suffer, that it joys in this. Oh, now there is occasion given to show that God respects me more, if I, for his sake, stand out in his quarrel, and break through all difficulties.

It will make us please him in all things that we are capable, in all things that we can do any way in our standings; as Christ describes it out of Moses, to 'love God with all our mind, with all our soul, and with all our strength,' Deut. vi. 5. Where love is, it sets all on work to please and give content. It sets the mind on work to study, Wherein shall I please God? And it will study God's truth, and not serve him by our own inventions. We must serve and love God after his mind; that is, as he hath commanded. It will set the wits on work to understand how he will be served, and to love him with all our soul, and with all our heart; that is, with the marrow and strength of our affections, with all my strength, be a man what he will be. If he be a magistrate, with the strength of his magistracy; if he be a minister, with the strength of his ministerial calling. In any condition I must love him, with all that that condition enableth me to. For it is a commanding affection; and being so, it commands all within and without to give content to the person loved. It commands the wit to devise, and the memory to retain, good things. It commands joy and delight; it commands anger to remove hindrances; and so all outward actions, love commands the doing of all things; it sets all on work. It is a most active affection. It is like to fire. It is compared to it. It sets all on work, and commands all that man is able to do. Therefore those that study not in all their endeavours according to their callings and places, according to every thing that God hath entrusted them with, to please God and to honour him in their conditions, they love not God.

What a shame is it, that when God hath given us such a sweet affection as love, that he should not have our love again, when we make ourselves happy in loving him? He is happy in his own love, the Father, Son, and Holy Ghost; but when he intends to make us happy, it is a shame that we should not bestow our affections upon him.

Much might be said to this purpose for the trial of ourselves, whether we love God or no. Let us not then forget these things; for it is the command both of the Old and New Testament; they run both upon love. 'I give you a new command,' saith Christ, John xv. 12; and yet it is no new command, but old and ordinary. But it is commanded now in the gospel; that is, it is renewed by new experiments[20] of God's love in Christ, 'that we should love him, as he hath loved us,' John xiii. 34, which is wonderfully; that we should love him, and 'love one another.' And all this is in this affection, as we see when the Holy Ghost would set out the disposition and qualification of such as those great things are prepared for, that 'neither eye hath seen, nor ear heard, nor hath entered into the heart of man,' he sets it down by this, 'They are for those that love him.'

---

20   That is, 'experiences' = 'manifestations.' — G.

# THE FOURTH SERMON

*As it is written, Eye hath not seen, nor ear heard, nor*
*hath entered into the heart of man, the things that God*
*hath prepared for them that love him.*
1 Cor. ii. 9.

That which hath already been said should force us to beg
the Spirit of God to teach the heart, to teach us the things
themselves, the inside of them. For a spiritual holy man
hath a spiritual knowledge of outward things of the creatures; he sees another manner of thing in the creature than
other men do. As another man hath a natural knowledge
of spiritual things, so a holy man hath a spiritual knowledge even of the ordinary works of God; and raiseth and
extracts a quintessence out of them, that a worldly man
cannot see, to glorify God, and to build up his faith in the
sense of God's favour, &c. This I add by the way to that.

But the highest performance of this, that there are
things provided for God's people that 'neither eye hath
seen nor ear hath heard,' &c., it is reserved for another world. For the promises of the gospel have then their
fulfilling indeed. These words are true of the state of the
gospel here now, but they have their accomplishment
in heaven. For whatsoever is begun here is ended there.
Peace begun here is ended there. Joy that is begun here it
shall be ended there. Communion of saints that is begun
here it shall be ended there. Sanctification that is begun
here it shall be ended there. So all graces shall be perfect,
and all promises performed then. That is the time indeed
when God shall discover things that 'neither eye hath seen
nor ear heard,' &c. In the mean time let us learn to believe them, and to live by faith in them, that there are such
things.

And God reserves not all for another world, but gives
his children a taste of those things beforehand to comfort
them in their distresses in this world, as indeed there is
nothing in this world of greater use and comfort to raise

them, than the beginnings of heaven upon earth. A little peace and joy in the Holy Ghost will make a man swallow all the discontents in the world. Now God is so far good to us, as that he lets us have some drops of these things beforehand to raise up our spirits, that by the taste we may know what great things he hath reserved for us. But of these things, and the use of them, I spoke before.

We come then to speak of the qualification of the persons.

'For them that love him.'

Not that we love God first, and then God prepares these things for us; but God prepares them, and acquaints us what he means to do with us, and then we love him. A Christian knows before what title he hath in Christ to heaven, and then he works. He knows Christ hath wrought salvation for him, and then he works out his salvation in a course tending to salvation. For there must be working in a course tending to the possession of salvation. That Christ hath purchased; we must not work and think by it to merit heaven. We know we have heaven, and those great things in the title of Christ, and then we fall on loving and working. There is a clean contrary order between us and those mercenaries. They invert the order of God; for, for whom God hath prepared these things, he discovers them to the eye of faith, and then faith works by love. This I add by the way.

Now he sets down this description of those persons for whom these excellent things are prepared, by this affection of love, by this grace of love, as being the fittest for that purpose to describe a Christian. Faith is not so fit, because it is not so discernible. We may know our love when we cannot know our faith. Ofttimes those that are excellent Christians, they doubt whether they believe or no; but ask them whether they love God and his truth and children or no? oh yes! they do. Now God intending to comfort us, sets out such an affection as a Christian may best discern; for of all affections we can discern best of our love. But to come to the affection itself, there are three things in love.

There is the affection, passion, grace of love. We speak of the grace here.

The affection is natural.

The passion is the excess of the natural affection when it overflows its bound.

Grace is the rectifying of the natural affection, and the elevating and raising it up to a higher object than nature can pitch on. The Spirit of God turns nature into grace, and works corruption and passion out of nature, and elevates and raiseth that which is naturally good, the affection of love to be a grace of love. He raiseth it up to love God (which nature cannot discover), by spiritualizing of it. He makes it the most excellent grace of all. So that while I speak of the love of God, think not that I speak of the mere affection, but of the affection that hath a stamp of grace upon it. For affections are graces when they are sanctified. And indeed all graces (set illumination aside, which is in the understanding) spring from this. What is true grace but joy, and love, and delight in the best things? And all others spring from love. What do we hate but what is opposite to that we love! And when are we angry, but when that we love is opposed and wronged? Then there is a holy zeal. So that indeed all grace is in the affections, and all affections are in this one primitive affection, this first-born and bred affection, love. I speak of it then as a special grace. Now the way of discerning of it we heard partly before. The way to discern of this sanctified affection, this grace, is to know what we esteem, for love, it is from an estimation. And likewise, in the second place, esteem breeds a desire of union. And desire of union breeds content in the thing when we have it. And contentment in the person breeds desire of contenting back again. These things I stood on, and will not press further.

Let us examine and try ourselves oft by our affections, how they stand biassed and pointed, whether to God and heavenward, or to the world; for we are as we love. For what we love, we, as it were, marry; and if we join our love to baser things, we marry baser things, and so debase ourselves. If we join in our affections to things above ourselves, to God, and spiritual things, we become spiritual as they are. So that a man stands in the world between two goods, somewhat that is better than himself, and something that is meaner; and thereafter as he joins in his affections, thereafter he is. For the affection of love to God and to the best things makes him excellent; and his affection to baser things makes him base. Let a man be never so base in the world, if his affections be base, he is a base person. Therefore we have the more need to try our affections.

But to answer some cases briefly.

1. It will be objected, may we not love anything but God and holy things? May we not love the creatures, because it is here specified as a note of those, that these

things are 'prepared for those that love God'?

Yes. We may love them as we see somewhat of God in them, as every creature hath somewhat of God in them. Whereupon God hath the style of every creature that hath good in it. He is called a 'Fountain,' a 'Rock,' a 'Shield,' everything that is good, to show that the creatures every one hath somewhat of God. He would not have taken the style of the creature else. We may love the creature as it hath somewhat of God in it, a being, or comfortable being, or somewhat; and as it conveys the love of God to us, and leads us back again to God. There is no creature but it conveys some love, and beams, and excellency of God to us in some kind, and leads us to God. So we may love other things. We may love men, and love God in them, and love them for God, to bring them to God, to leave a holy impression in them, to be like God. There is no question of this. But the love of God, that is the spring of all.

But it will be said by some weak conscience, How shall I know I love God, when I love the world and worldly things? I love my children, and other things, perhaps that are not ill; I fear I love them more than God.

We must know for this, that when two streams run in one channel they run stronger than one stream. When a man loves other good things, nature goes with grace. So nature, going with grace, the stream is strong. But when a man loves God, and Christ, and heavenly things, there is grace only; nature yields nothing to that. When a man loves his children or his intimate friends, &c., nature going with grace, it is no wonder if the stream be stronger when two streams run in one. So corruption in ill action ofttimes carry the affections strong. As in many of our loves there is somewhat natural that is good, yet there is some corruption, as to love a man for ill. Here nature and corruption is strong, but in supernatural things grace goes alone.

Then again, we must not judge by an indeliberate passion, by what our affection is carried suddenly and indeliberately to; for so we may joy more in a sudden thing than in the best things of all, as in the sight of a friend there may be a sudden affection. But the love of God, it is a constant stream. It is not a torrent, but a current that runs all our lifetime. Therefore those affections to God and heavenly things, in a Christian, they are perpetual. They make no great noise, perhaps, but they are perpetual in the heart of a Christian. A sudden torrent and passion may transport a man, but yet he may have a holy and heavenly heart. I speak this for comfort.

2. Ay, but my love to God is faint and little.

Well, but it is a heavenly spark, and hath divinity in it. It is from heaven, and is growing, and vigorous, and efficacious: and a little heavenly love will waste all carnal love at length, it is of so vigorous and constant a nature. It is fed still by the Spirit; and a little that is fed and maintained, that is growing, that hath a blessing in it (as the love of God in the hearts of his hath; for God continually cherisheth his own beginning), that little shall never be quenched, but shall overgrow nature at length, and eat out corruption, and all contrary love whatsoever. Though for the present we see corruption overpower and oppress grace, yet the love of God being a divine spark, and therefore being more powerful, though it be little, than the contrary, it hath a blessing in it to grow, till at length it consume all. For love is like fire; as in other properties so in this, it wastes and consumes the contrary; and raiseth up to heaven, and quickens, and enlivens the persons, as fire doth. And it makes lightsome dead bodies; it transforms them all into fire like itself. So the love of God, by little and little, transforms us all to be fiery; it transforms us to be lovers. These cases needed a little touching, to satisfy some that are good and growing Christians, and must have some satisfaction.

3. But it may he asked again, as indeed we see it is true, what is the reason that sometime meaner Christians have more loving souls than great scholars, men of great parts? One would think that knowledge should increase love and affection?

So it doth, if it be a clear knowledge; but great wits and pates,[21] and great scholars busy themselves about questions and intricacies, and so they are not so much about the affections. A poor Christian ofttimes takes those things for granted that they study, and dispute, and canvass, and question. There is a heavenly light in his soul that God is my Father in Christ, and Christ, God and man, is my Mediator. He takes it for granted, and so his affections are not troubled. Whereas the other, having corruption answerable to his parts, great wit and great corruption, he is tangled with doubts and arguments. He studies to inform his brain; the other to be heated in his affections. A poor Christian cares not for cold niceties, that heat not the heart and affections; he takes these for granted if they

---

21  That is, 'heads.' — G.

be propounded in the Scripture. Instead of disputing, he believes, and loves, and obeys; and that is the reason that many a poor soul goes to heaven with a great deal of joy, when others are tangled and wrapped in their own doubts. So much for satisfying of these things. To go on, therefore, to give a few directions how to have this heavenly fire kindled in us, to love God, considering such great things are provided for those that love God. It is a matter of consequence: as we desire heaven, we must desire this holy fire to be kindled in us.

Let us know for a ground, as it were, that it is our duty to aim at the highest pitch of love that we can, and not to rest in the lowest. The lowest pitch of loving God, is to love God because he is good to us. That is good. The Scriptures stoops so low as to allow that God would have us love him and holy things for the benefit we have by them. But that is mercenary if we rest there. But God stoops to allure us by promises and favours, though we must not rest there. But we must love God, not for ourselves, but labour to rise to this pitch, to love ourselves in God, and to see that we have happiness in God, and not in ourselves. Our being is in him. We must love ourselves in him, and be content to be lost in God; that is, so to love God, that if he should cast us away (his kindness is better than life), do others what they will, we will love him, and ourselves for his excellencies, and because we see ourselves in him and are his children. We must labour to rise to that, and that is the highest pitch that we can attain to. We must know that for a ground.

And know this for another, that when we speak of the love of God, we speak of love incorporate into our conversations and actions; not of an abstracted love and affection, but of love in our places, and callings, and standings, love invested into action. Therefore the Scripture saith, we must love God 'with all our mind, with all our heart, with all our power and strength,' Deut. vi. 5; that is, in our particular places. To make it clear. When we speak of love to God, we speak of love to him in our particular callings. He loves God that is a magistrate and executes justice for God's sake; and he that is a minister, and teacheth the people conscionably for God's sake, and shows them the way to heaven. He loves God as a man in the commonwealth, a statesman, &c., that in that place seeks the glory of God, and the good of the church and religion. Shall men talk of love to God, and their affections are stirred up I know not whereabout? No. It is an affection that is discovered in actions.

How can we love God with all our might, except as far as our might extends, our love extends? How far doth thy activity, thy power, thy sphere, that thou canst do anything, stretch? So far must thy love; and thou must show thy love in all the powers and abilities that God hath furnished thee with.

For a man that hath great place and opportunity to do good, and to think it enough only to love God in his closet, &c., this is not the love we speak of. A man must love God with all his might, as he stands invested in relation this way or that way.

The love of God in a private man will not serve for a magistrate or a public man. He must show his love in his place by standing in the gap, to hinder all the ill, and to do all the good he can. Every man must do so, but such a one more especially, because God hath trusted him with more. Well, these things premised, to come to some directions how to come to love God.

First of all, the way to love God *is to have a heavenly light to discover what we are in ourselves and our emptiness*; for being as we are, we can never love God till we see in what need we stand of his favour and grace, that we are damned creatures else.

Now when we come to have our eyes opened to see our sinfulness and emptiness, we will make out to God, and make out to his mercy in Christ above all things. Indeed, the first love is the love of dependence, before we come to a love of friendship and complacency with God; a love to go out to him, and to depend upon him for mercy and grace and all. A love that riseth from the sense of our misery, and goes to him for supply.

There is a sweet concurrence of misery and mercy; of emptiness and fulness; of beggary and riches.

Now when we see our own misery, and beggary, and sinfulness; and then a fulness in God to supply; of riches to enrich us every way; then this breeds a love. This is the way to all other loves that follow. And where this is not premised, and goes before, a man will never delight in God. In Luke vii. 47 that good woman she loved much. Why? Much was forgiven her; many sins were forgiven her.

So when the soul shall see what need it hath of forgiving mercy, of pardoning mercy, and how many great debts God hath forgiven us in Christ, there will be a great deal of love, because there is a great deal forgiven. And we must begin indeed with seeing the infinite mercy of God before any other attribute of God, and then we shall love him after. This is the first thing. There is no soul that over loves God so, as the poor soul that hath been abased with the sense of sin and its emptiness, that it is empty of all goodness; and then sees a supply in the mercy of God in Christ. Those souls love God above all.

Another way to love God is to consider of his wonderful goodness, to meditate and think of it. He is good and doth good. It is a communicative goodness. Let us think of his goodness, and the streaming of it out to the creature. The whole earth is full of the goodness of the Lord. What are all the creatures but God's goodness? We can see nothing but the goodness of God. What is all the creatures but *Deus explicatus*, God unfolded to our senses? He offers himself to our bodies and souls; all is God's goodness.

And then see this goodness fitted to us. It is a fit goodness that comes from God. He is good and doth good, and so fitly he proportions his goodness. For he hath fitted every part of us, soul and body, with goodness; all the senses with goodness. What do we see but goodness in colours? What do we hear but his good, in those delights that come that way? We taste and feel his goodness. Against the cold we have clothing; in hunger we have food; in all necessities, in all exigencies, we have fit considerations of God for all necessities whatsoever outward.

But then for our souls, what food hath he for that? The death of Christ, his own Son, to feed our souls. The soul is a spiritual substance; and he thought nothing good enough to feed it but his own Son. We feed on God's love in giving Christ to death; and on Christ's love in giving himself to death.

The soul being continually troubled with the guilt of some sin or other, it feeds on this; it is nourished with Christ every day more and more, especially at the sacrament. Thus we see how God hath fitted his goodness to us. And then in particular dangers how he fits us with several deliverances; so seasonably as we may see God's love in it.

Then as God's goodness is great and fit, so it is near us. It is not a goodness afar off, but God follows us with his goodness in whatsoever condition we he. He applies himself to us, and he hath taken upon him near relations, that he might be near us in goodness. He is a father, and everywhere to maintain us. He is a husband, and everywhere to help. He is a friend, and everywhere to comfort and counsel. So his love it is a near love. Therefore he hath taken upon him the nearest relations, that we may never want God and the testimonies of his love.

And then again this goodness of God, which is the object of love, it is a free goodness, merely from himself; and an overflowing goodness, and an everlasting goodness. It is never drawn dry; he loves us unto life everlasting. He loves us in this world, and follows us with signs of his love in all the parts of us, in body and soul, till he hath brought body and soul to heaven to enjoy himself for ever there. These and such like considerations may serve to stir us up to love God, and direct us how to love God.

Benefits will work upon a beast; as it is Isaiah i. 2, 'Hear, O heavens; and hearken, O earth: the ox knoweth his owner, and the ass his master's crib; but my people have forgotten me.'

Proud men become baser, and more brute than the very brutes; benefits will move the very brute creatures. So, I say, these favours to us in particular should move us, except we will be more brute than the brutes themselves.

Especially to move us all, consider some particularities of favours to us more than to others, for specialties do much increase love and respect.

*Consider how God hath followed thee with goodness outwardly, when others have been neglected.* Thou hast a place in the world, and riches, and friends, when many other excellent persons want all these. There are some common favours to all Christians; as the favour we have in Christ, forgiveness of sins, sanctification, and such other favours. But there be some specialties of divine providence, whereby it appears that God's providence hath watched over us in some particulars more than others; those be special engagements. And is there any of us that cannot say that God hath dealt specially, in giving them some mercy more than to others? I add this therefore to the rest.

Again, to help us to stir up this grace of love, *consider those examples of loving of those that have then lived in former times.* Take David, and Paul, and other holy men. David wonders at his own love: 'Lord, how do I love thy law!' Ps. cxix. 97. And have we not more cause comparing the grounds of our affection, when we have more than they in those times? What! did he wonder at his love of God's law, when the canon was so short? They had only Moses, and some few books, and we have the canon enlarged; we

have both the Old and New Testament, shall not we say
much more, How do I love thy law, thy gospel, and divine
truths! This should shame us, when they in dark times so
loved the truth of God, and we see all clear and open, and
yet are cold.

Likewise it is good in this case to *converse with those
that are affectionate*. As face answereth face, so spirit an-
swers spirit; as 'iron sharpeneth iron,' so one sharpens
another, Prov. xxvii. 17. Conversation with cold ones will
make one cold: 'For the abundance of iniquity, the love of
many shall wax cold,' Matt. xxiv. 12. Conversing with sinful, cold people casts a damp upon us. But let us labour, if
we will be wise for our souls, when we find any coldness
of affection, to converse with those that have sweet and
heavenly affections. It will marvellously work upon our
hearts.

I might say much this way to stir us up, and direct us
how to love God.

But indeed nothing will so much enable us to love
God as a new nature. Nature will love without provoca-
tion. The fire will burn, because it is fire; and the water
will moisten, because it is water; and a holy man will love
holy things, because he is holy; a spiritual soul will love
spiritual things, because he is spiritual. Therefore, besides
all, add this, that our natures be changed more and more,
that they be sanctified and circumcised as God hath prom-
ised: 'I will circumcise your hearts, that ye may love me,'
Deut. xxx. 6. There must be a circumcised heart to love
God. We must be sanctified to love God; for if nature is
not renewed, there cannot be this new commandment of
love. Why is love called a new commandment, and an old
commandment?

It is called old for the letter, because it was a command
in Moses time: 'Thou shalt love the Lord with all thy soul,'
Deut. vi. 5. But now it is a new commandment, because
there is abundance of spirit given by Christ; and the Spirit
sanctifies us and writes this affection in our hearts. It was
written in stone before, but now is written in our hearts by
the Spirit. And now there are new incentives and motives
to love, since Christ came and gave himself for us, new
encouragements and provocations to love. Therefore it is a
new commandment, from new grounds and motions, that
are more a great deal than before Christ. But there must be
a now heart to obey this new command of love. The old
heart will never love.

Therefore we must, with all the means that may be used, beg the Spirit of sanctification especially, beg the discovery of God's love to us, for our love is but a reflection of God's love. We cannot love God except he love us first. Now, our love being a reflection of God's love, we must desire that he would give us his Spirit to reveal his love; that the Spirit being a witness of God's love to us, may thereupon be a Spirit of love and sanctification in us.

And let us labour to grow more in the assurance of God's love, and all the evidences of it. Let us dwell long in the meditation of these things. The dwelling in the meditation of God's love, it will make us to love him again. As many beams in a burning-glass meeting together they cause a fire, many thoughts of the many fruits of God's love in this world, and what he intends us in the world to come, our hearts dwelling on them, these beams will kindle a holy fire in our hearts.

Many are troubled with cold affections, and wish, Oh that they could love! They forget the way how to love. They will not meditate; and if they do meditate, they think to work love out of their own hearts. They may as well work fire out of a flint, and water out of a stone. Our hearts are a barren wilderness. Therefore let us beg the Spirit that God would alter our hearts, with meditation and all other helps; that God would sanctify us, and discover his love to us, and that he would give us his Spirit (for he doth the one where he doth the other). When God doth so, then we shall be enabled to love him. We must not think to bring love to God, but we must fetch love from God. We must light our candle at his fire. Think of his love to us, and beg the Spirit of love from him; love is a fruit of the Spirit. That is the course we ought to take, for God will teach our hearts to love.

Now, to stir us up the more, to add some motives and encouragements to labour more to get this affection. Let us consider seriously that without this love of God we are dead; and whatsoever comes from us it is stillborn, it is dead. Without love we are nothing; without love all that comes from us is nothing; without love 'I am as a tinkling cymbal,' saith Paul, 1 Cor. xiii. 1. For a man to be nothing in religion, and all that comes from him to be dead and still-born, to be abortive actions, who would be in such a case? Therefore let us labour, before we do anything that is good, to have our hearts kindled with the love of God, and then we shall be somebody, and that that we do will be acceptable; for love sweetens all performances. It is not the action, but the love in the action; as from God it is not the dead favour that comes from him that comforts the soul of a Christian, so much as the love and sweetness of God in the favour. That is better than the thing itself. When we have favour from God in outward favours, consider the sweetness: 'Taste and see how gracious the Lord is,' Ps. xxxiv. 8. The taste of the love and favour of God in the blessing is better than the thing itself, for it is but a dead thing. And so from us back again to God. What are the things we perform to him? They are dead. But when they are sweetened with the affection of love, done to him as a father in Christ, he tastes our performances as sweet. Love makes all we do to have a relish, and all that he doth to us. Therefore we should labour for this sweet affection.

And withal consider, that we may be called to do many things in this world. Surely there are none of us but we have many holy actions to perform. We have many things to suffer and endure in the world, many temptations to resist. What shall or will carry us through all? Nothing but love. If we have loving and gracious hearts, this affection will carry us through all good actions, through all oppositions and temptations; for 'love is strong as death,' Cant. viii. 6. Consider therefore that there are so many things that will require this affection, this blessed wing and wind of the soul, to carry us along, in spite of all that is contrary, through all opposition; *let us labour for love, and that affection will carry us through all*. Indeed, if we have that it is no matter what a man suffers. A man can never be miserable that hath this affection of love. If this heavenly fire be kindled in him he cannot be miserable; take him in what condition you will, take him upon the rack. St Paul in the dungeon sang at midnight in the dungeon, in the stocks, at an uncomfortable time and place. When he had been misused, his heart was enlarged to sing to God out of love, Acts xvi. 25. Nay, everything increaseth it. The things we suffer increaseth this flame. Let a man love God, whatsoever he suffers in a good cause it increaseth his love, he shall find his love increased with it. The more he loves the more he can suffer; and the more he suffers the more he loves God, and the more he increaseth in a joyful expectation of the times to come. And love is alway with joy, and hope, and other sweet affections. It draws joy with it always, and hope of better things; and as joy increaseth and hope increaseth, so a man's happiness increaseth in this world. Therefore it is no matter what a man suffers that hath a gracious and loving heart, enlarged by the Spirit of God. Let him never think of what he suffereth of pain, of losses and crosses, if God discover his fatherly breast, and shine on him in Christ; and he look on God reconciled, and taste of the joys of heaven beforehand. If you tell him of sufferings, you tell him of that that encourageth him. It is an argument I might be long in, and to great purpose; for if we get this holy fire kindled once, we shall need little exhortation to other duties. It would set us on work to all. And like the fire of the sanctuary that never went out, so it is such an affection, that if it be once kindled in the heart it will never out. It is a kind of miracle in ill when we love other things besides God, baser than ourselves; it is as much as if a river should turn backward. For man that is an excellent creature, to be carried with the stream of his affection to things worse than himself, it is a kind of monster for a man to abuse his understanding so. What a base thing is it for a man to suffer such a sweet stream as love, a holy current, to run into a sink? Who would turn a sweet stream into a sink, and not rather into a garden? Into a sweet place to refresh that? Our love is the best thing in the world, and who deserves it better than God and Christ? We can never return anything, but this affection of love we may again. And can we place it better than upon divine things, whereby we are made better ourselves? Doth God require our affections for himself? No. It is to make us happy. It advanceth our affection to love him; it is the turning of it into the right stream. It is the making of us happy that God requires it. For consider all things that may deserve this affection. It will keep us from all sin. What is any sin but the abuse of love? For the crookedness of this affection turns us to present things, that is the cause of all sin. For what is all sin, but pleasure and honours and profits, the three idols of the world? All sin is about them. And what are all good actions but love well placed? The well ordering of this affection is the well ordering of our lives; and the misplacing of this affection is the cause of all sin.

And to make us the more careful this way, consider that when we place our affections upon anything else, consider the vanity of it. We lose our love and the thing and ourselves. For whatsoever else we love, if we love not God in it, and love it for God, it will perish and come to nothing ere long. The affection perisheth with the thing. We lose our affections and the thing; and lose ourselves too, mis-

placing of it. These are forcible considerations with understanding persons. And if we would use our understanding
and consideration and meditation, and our souls, as we
should, to consider of the grounds and encouragements
we have to love God, and the best things whereby we may
be dignified above ourselves, it would not be as it is; we
should not be so devoid of grace and comfort. It was a miracle that the three young men should be in the midst of
the furnace, and be there as if they were in another place,
no hotter, Dan. iii. 12, 13, *seq*. And it is a miracle that men
should be in the midst of all encouragements that we have
to love God (as there is not the like reasons for anything
in the world to keep our souls in a perpetual heat of affection to love God—no motives, or arguments, or incentives;
all are nothing to the multitude of arguments we have to
inflame our affections), and yet to be cold in the midst of
the fire. It is a kind of miracle to have dark understandings
and dead affections; that notwithstanding all the heavenly
means we have to keep a perpetual flame of love to God,
yet to be cold and dark in our souls; let us bewail it and be
ashamed of it.

What do we profess ourselves? Christians, heirs of
heaven; so beloved of God as that he gave his own Son to
deliver us, being rebels and enemies, in so cursed a state
as we are all in by nature. Poor creature! Inferior to the
angels that fell, that he should love man, sinful dust and
ashes, so much as to give his own Son to free us from so
great misery, and to advance us to so great happiness, to
set us in 'heavenly places with Christ,' Eph. i. 3, and to
have perpetual communion with him in heaven; to have
such encouragements, and to be cold and dead-hearted;
nay, wilfully opposite in our affections, to be enemies to
the goodness of God and grace, having such arguments
to love God. And yet how many spirits edged by the devil
oppose all that is good, and will not give way to God's
Spirit? God would have them temples, they will be sties.
God would marry them; nay, they will be harlots. God
would have them happy here, and hereafter. No; they will
not; they will have their own lusts and affections.

Let us be afraid of these things, as we love our own
souls and ourselves; and consider what encouragements
we have to love God for which such great things are reserved as 'neither eye hath seen, nor ear heard, nor hath
entered into the heart of man to conceive.'

88380857R00045

Made in the USA
Columbia, SC
29 January 2018